DEDICATION

To my friends among the farmers, keepers, stalkers and countrymen generally who have taught me not only all I know of shooting but, unknowingly, much about the art of living happily.

CONTENTS

ILLUSTRATIONS

ALL PHOTOGRAPHS WERE TAKEN BY THE AUTHOR

ACKNOWLEDGEMENTS

My thanks are due to the following:

To Gough Thomas for drawing the illustration of a gun on page 39.
To the Eley Ammunition Division of Imperial Metal Industries, Ltd.
for the illustration of a cartridge on page 43.
To Peter Turner, the Honorary Legal Adviser to WAGBI, for vetting
the Chapter on Shooting and the Law.
To Charles Coles of the Game Conservancy, and the very practical
publications of that organization.
To the editors of the *Shooting Times* and *The Field* for permission to
reproduce some of my photographs which have previously appeared
in their publications.
To my wife and the *Good Housekeeping Cookery Book* whose skills I
sought in writing the chapter on cooking the quarry.

FOREWORD
SALUTE TO THE AUTHOR

Great sweeps of Derbyshire grouse moor met the schoolboy gaze of Marchington J. in the summer of 1944, that summer of sacrifice and rising hopes. Across the Channel the German armies were being smashed time and again. It was a bad time to be young and out of it. Across the road some of those temporarily disengaged from World War II were shooting on and after August 12, tiny distant dots receding even further into the purple spaces of the ling.

To Marchington J., then aged fourteen, the two circumstances had their message. The family was not flush; a bookmaker would have laid long odds against his ever setting foot on a grouse moor except as a beater. But he had a logical mind and logic admitted no reason why a man who sincerely wanted one, and who acquitted himself well in all spheres of life, should not in due course be the man in possession. The second World War was ending in victory. Better days lay ahead. To a man of fourteen it was time to be up and doing, keeping an eye meanwhile on the things that make life worth living.

The years have rolled by. Events, largely of his own making, have combined to place Marchington J. in the situation which he foresaw so long ago. He has taken his moor, entertained his friends, had his share of pheasants and partridges, of wildfowl, and all the fun and under-rated fringe benefits of 'the rough'. The sturdy gritstone cottage beside the high Peakland road is a receding memory; but unforgotten (as is most else which has happened in the meantime). It delivers him from the evil of pretended grandeur.

Mr. Marchington is now 43. In early middle age he is still younger than most men who in the past have written books about shooting. It will have been noted that he came to the sport by what must be for many an untraditional route.

Because his approach was different his book is also different. The supposed authority which has led many to appear in print has generally been based on expertise fortified by seniority. So the possibility has often existed that writers on shooting have parted company, as it were, with their own beginnings. Perhaps, also they absorbed their basic knowledge during those enviable school holidays in more stay-at-home times than these, when they were turned out with the keeper for weeks on end to breathe in the lore of the woods and the moors, absorbing it all as only the young can, without really knowing that absorption is taking place.

Such legacies of almost instinctive knowledge, precious as they are, are becoming rarer nowadays, through lack of opportunity to acquire them. It is fair to add that those who have inherited such knowledge have not always realized that inheritance is not universal, and have assumed a shared knowledge which their readers did not possess. But Marchington, who learned about shooting and the countryside and its wildlife, during years of conscious experience, is writing out of the same background as most of his readers will have known.

If this makes his approach specially valuable, there is something else to multiply this value. This is the presence, not in the background of his life but very much in its foreground, of his three sons and two daughters and his wife, all of whom learn from him (inevitably with their own varying slants and interests) of the things which he details in this book. One cannot explain to children without encountering the reiterated 'Why?', nor can one avoid the obligation of giving a clear and comprehensible answer, for cross-examination continues until one does. This is probably the reason for the exceptional clarity of the chapters which follow. Nothing is merely asserted; everything is explained; there is no talking-down; neither is there dogma for its own sake.

In another fundamental respect the Marchington approach differs from that of most of his predecessors. He recognizes, as he must since he is himself one of the products of it, the fusion of the urban and rural society which has taken place in his lifetime. To be a countryman is no longer a matter of place of residence and occupation. It is a matter of attitude of mind, of where one's heart is.

Very genuine countrymen escape from the asphalt cities for a few brief hours every weekend. There are instinctive townsmen operating factory farms, interested in their surroundings only for their money. So Marchington does not encounter that pitfall which has trapped so many others. The implication that those who must live in town are in some way inferior beings, unfit or unable to know the whole truth about nature and the outdoor world, has no place with him. This is an age of commutation, of shifting populations, of declining numbers in the farming community; there are few enough who truly merit the title of countrymen as it was understood a generation ago. In writing for society as it is actually structured today Marchington has done something new.

When the reader puts his book down at the end of the last chapter I believe he will share my view that Marchington has attained his objective completely, faithfully and gracefully. The judgment which has stood him in good stead in many spheres gives balance to his arguments and his conclusions about this great and growing sport. The joy which he gains not merely from gun, dog and camera, but from wildlife and the elements in their simplest forms, lights up those passages which might have been mere routine. His insistence on excellence in all that he does (never better exemplified than in the superb photographs, all taken by himself) ensures that the Marchington influence will precipitate no slipping of standards.

Perhaps this will become a standard work on the sport of shooting in the twentieth century. Certainly it will be memorable. These predictions are made with confidence, if with the discount which is due from a friend. Now it is for his readers to form their own opinion. I have had no fear of recording mine.

WILSON STEPHENS   EDITOR OF The Field

INTRODUCTION

There are many forms of shooting carried out with many different varieties of weapons but this book is concerned with the most common interpretation, the sport of shooting wild creatures with smooth bore shotguns.

For countless years men pursued wild life in order to live, and failure could mean death from starvation. As a result the instinct to hunt, fish and shoot is a strong one which even the sophisticated life of our cities has merely glossed over. For many people, even town dwellers, the sight of a cock pheasant rising from a wood, the first lunge of a hooked fish, or the cry of hounds will bring a stab of excitement that has its roots in our primitive past.

Contrary to the belief of people who know nothing of the sport, the main object of shooting is not killing wild life. Of course the sport involves killing, and many people object to it for this reason. This is an important issue, and I have devoted part of a chapter to it at the beginning of the book. But there are many other aspects and subsidiary interests of the sport. The man who takes up shooting will learn a great deal about the countryside and its wild life. He will learn the numerous tricks of both comfort and survival, not only in the great range of weather conditions we encounter in these Islands, but in lesser matters such as coping with Scottish midges. There are many other crafts to be acquired - concealment, moving quietly, developing a sense of direction, map reading, preparing game birds for the table, dog training, ferret breeding - the list is endless.

On a broader scale shooting encourages quick reactions and keen observation. It also calls for rapid decision-making when, occasionally, the wrong one could mean not just an empty game bag but a wetting on the marsh or a night spent on the hills. But of all the advantages I can list for shooting the most important is that it gets people into the countryside. There is about country people a wholesomeness, a healthy soundness of character, a tranquillity of mind, that is absent from most city dwellers and it stems from close contact with nature. In an increasingly artificial age any sport that takes the participant outdoors is to be encouraged and none does this better than shooting.

It is quite impossible to convey the enormous wealth of knowledge on shooting within a single book, and in places I have recommended books concerned with specialist subjects. Additionally I would commend to the reader the two weekly publications *The Field* and *The Shooting Times*, for within their highly authoritative pages all the shooting wisdom of the ages has appeared in the past and will appear again.

The two organizations concerned with promoting and defending the interests of the sport are the Wildfowlers' Association of Great Britain and Ireland, popularly known as WAGBI, and the British Field Sports Society. WAGBI's name is deceptive for although it was created in 1908 to further the sport of wildfowling it is now concerned with all forms of sporting shooting and conservation. It is a most vigorous organization and merits the support of every shooting man. Details can be had from the Headquarters at Grosvenor House, Watergate Street, Chester. As you progress through this book it will become obvious that I am a strong WAGBI supporter, and I make no apology for this. I serve on the Management Committee of the Association and no one listening to the deliberations of a meeting could fail to be impressed by the enormous scope of WAGBI's activities and the great energy and enthusiasm of both the permanent officers and the numerous honorary workers. The Association has grown to its present stature, both in size and authority, because past and present generations of shooting men have believed in the need for a representative body for the sport. But for the efforts of WAGBI and BFSS the sport of shooting might now be non-existent or followed on a much restricted scale, and I am of the opinion that every shooting man should belong to at least one and preferably both organizations. When the sport is attacked there is always an influx of new members who, having been sitting outside for the last decade or so, send in their subscription and immediately start asking what is being done to protect their interests. This is not good enough. It takes years to build up a strong and influential organization, and support, both in numbers and finance, is needed at all times, not least because the work ranges far more widely than the mainly negative function of protection.

As the name implies the BFSS is concerned with the defence and promotion of all forms of field sports, and, while its activities are far ranging, it is most active on the political scene. For this reason much of its best work goes unseen, but this should not deceive you into thinking the Society does not justify your support. The address is 137, Victoria Street, London, S.W.1.

This book is written for newcomers to the sport, and I have tried to give not only practical advice but to instil the right attitudes towards the quarry, the countryside, and the people who live in it. I hope the sport of shooting brings you the great pleasure it has given me, both from the sport and the many people and places to which it has led me.

Chapter 1

A SHOOTING PHILOSOPHY

The majority of authors of books on shooting have given priority to the practical aspects of the sport, and plunged immediately into the technicalities of what to shoot with and how to hit the target. My own belief is that the degree of success in terms of game in the bag is of much less importance than the attitude of mind with which one pursues the sport. Very, very few experienced shooting men shoot because they derive any pleasure from the act of killing. Their reasons vary but all of them enjoy their sport because of the side issues involved, and I think it will assist newcomers to gain the maximum pleasure from shooting if I devote this chapter to considering some of the less practical but in many ways more important issues.

Until quite recently life for the majority of men was harsh, and this was reflected in their treatment of the other creatures both wild and domesticated. Few people concerned themselves with the moral rights and wrongs of killing for sport, and even fewer with the need to conserve the countryside and its wildlife. In fact the need for conservation has become a matter of extreme urgency only within the last few decades as the pressures of an increasing population and modern technology have combined. Shooting also enjoyed a considerable degree of built-in protection from criticism from the fact that many of the most influential people of the past were landowners, and as such they were either shooting men or familiar with the sport. With the decline of the large estates and the rapid growth of both education and power among the masses, opposition to all the field sports, popularly grouped under the title of blood sports, grew. Unfortunately in recent years much time and effort has gone into both attacking and defending field sports which would have been far better spent in protecting rapidly shrinking countryside, although recently the urgent need for conservation has been more widely realized.

23

As a result many organizations are playing a part in all the various aspects of conservation and shooting men are no exception. Conservation can involve many aspects of protection, from fighting for cleaner rivers, or opposing the proposed line of a new motorway, to some such simple action as planting a new tree to replace one felled. In terms of shooting the work of the Wildfowlers' Association is a fine example, for the majority of the 200 plus affiliated clubs each contribute in some way towards a comprehensive conservation policy. Many of these have created their own local reserves in which shooting is either limited or completely banned, and the members have reared many tens of thousands of duck. WAGBI has developed its own conservation centre from a long disused duck decoy at Boarstall, Bucks, and this is well worth a visit. There are many other ways in which the Association and its members are active conservationists, as a brief study of any of the Associations' literature will show. But WAGBI is only one of a considerable number of organizations wholly or partly concerned with conservation, and these range through such formidable bodies as the Wildfowl Trust, the Royal Society for Protection of Birds, the National Trust and the Nature Conservancy to various international organizations. With this impressive total of support for the cause of conservation you might well feel that they can be left to get on with the job while you concentrate on shooting. You would be wrong. The exponents of the cause may be strong but the task they face is immense; so immense that it is not so much a question of trying to succeed as minimizing the impact. We must have more houses, roads, schools, and all the ancillary growth that goes with them, but a great deal can be done to see that development is controlled so as to do the least harm to the countryside. The great danger is apathy, not on the part of the conservation bodies but of individuals. It is very easy to feel that you are only a lone voice and can do nothing, but if everyone feels the same the conservation movement will collapse through lack of grass root support. There is a moral obligation on everyone who gains pleasure from the countryside to do all they can to protect it.

As the purchaser of a book for newcomers to shooting there is a strong probability that you have not, as yet, shot a living creature, and when you do your conscience may well ask some searching questions.

▲1 A fine example of an old 4-bore hammer gun by Tolley. Note the under-lever opening. the cone-shaped top extension and, most unusually, leaf rear sights. These would be used for long-range shots at sitting targets.

▼2 Teaching a boy to shoot with clay pigeons. An experienced instructor can usually tell the pupil where the shot went.

▲3 This is an excellent shooting position. The butt is well up in the shoulder so the eye can look along the rib without the head being dipped uncomfortably. The left arm is almost straight and the hand nicely under the barrels.

▼4 Most novices make the mistake of leaning back instead of keeping their weight on the front foot. Here the instructor is preventing this error. The boy's left hand should be further along the barrels.

▲5 The Gun prepares for an oncoming cock pheasant. The tips of the barrels lie on a line between the eyes and the target. The body is pivoting from the hips and as the bird nears the butt will slide up to the shoulder.

▼6 Practice at clay pigeons is very valuable and only requires a simple trap and an assistant.

▲7 The barrels have followed the flight path of the pigeon and accelerated until they lead the target. The gun will discharge now.

▼8 This photograph shows the two spent cartridges being kicked clear by the ejector mechanism.

If so, this is a good thing, for I would expect most thinking men to have some qualms over the act of killing. I still vividly recall my first day's pigeon decoying when I shot some thirty birds, and as the pile of dead mounted so did my mental reservations. Since that time I have killed thousands of creatures, and slowly I have developed a philosophy which is born of a love of shooting on the one hand, and what I like to regard as a basically kind and sympathetic nature on the other. In time your own views will crystallize, but at this stage it will at least give you food for thought if you know mine.

The progress of society has meant that all activities that are harmful to wild creatures have come under close examination, and in most cases, criticism. Shooting is no exception to this, and is under constant attack by the two organizations which are popularly regarded as the anti-blood sports societies. The constant verbal war which endures between the followers of field sports on the one hand, and their opponents on the other is not, unfortunately, outstanding for the quality of debate, but really this is unavoidable as the object of the attacks and counter attacks is not to convert the other side but to sway the great British public, the majority of whom are apathetic to the whole issue. At least, that is, until a war starts, when suddenly men who can handle a gun, and are at home in the countryside, are in great demand. As a beginning you must not make the mistake of dismissing the opponents of field sports as bigoted idiots. The noisy spear-head may perhaps appear ill-informed and prejudiced, but beyond them there are many worthy men and women who feel strongly that it is wrong to kill. I find it very reassuring that when I talk to such people they are almost invariably townspeople who know little of shooting. Country folk who are nearer by far to nature, and who see the natural flow of life and death more closely, rarely object to shooting even if they are non-shooters themselves. But let us examine the arguments of the opposition. Fundamentally they say that men should not kill wild creatures for sport. The first portion of this argument, that men should not kill wild creatures, is easily defeated. Whenever I get involved in such a verbal tussle I ask the opposition what he or she has eaten that day, and the reply nearly always encompasses such items as bacon, lamb and other innocent creatures. Quite obviously the only person who can argue against killing wild creatures without being a hypocrite must be a vegetarian. There is even an excellent defence against rearing pheasants for shooting, for what is the difference between this practise and rearing turkeys for Christmas, or any other livestock. In fact I would rather be reborn as a gamekeeper's pheasant chick than a turkey, for as a pheasant I would at least be set free, and have a chance of survival. As a turkey I would be doomed.

Looked at from this angle there is no problem in defending shooting, and indeed the attack of many of the opponents ends here. But for the deeper thinkers the words 'for sport' must be considered. Man must kill to live, whether it is livestock on the land or fish in the sea, but the majority of the human killers do it for a living whereas we shooting men kill for pleasure. There is a simple defence that it is better to kill for pleasure than for money, as do the others, but this merely side steps the question. The answer, at least in my case, is that I do not kill for pleasure – I hunt for pleasure, and the process involves the death of the quarry. I am fulfilling an age old instinct, for men have hunted since time immortal. One can justify this by showing that the whole pattern of nature depends upon superior species preying upon lesser species. The deeper thinkers among the antis might reply that as men we should raise ourselves above the brutalities of nature, and here they have a point. But I enjoy my sport, and provided I can carry it out without causing more than an occasional minimum of distress or suffering to the quarry, I am satisfied that I can continue shooting with a clear conscience. I do not pretend that shooting is a sport above criticism, but when I weigh the good and the bad the scales fall heavily on the right side.

This reasoning is valid only if I am correct in my belief that the degree of distress and suffering experienced by the quarry is non-existent or slight. Let us consider if this is so, and begin with the perfect example of a duck flighting at dusk. I kill it cleanly before it even realizes that I am there – it has suffered neither pain nor apprehension. But, the antis reply, most quarries are aware of the presence of the hunters and terrified of them. This statement makes sense only if we consider it in terms of human understanding, and it is this shallow and emotional thinking which sets most opponents of shooting off on the wrong track. Wild creatures cannot reason; their actions are motivated by instinct and conditioned reflexes. There exists ample scientific proof of this statement, but if you think about it for a moment your own experience will show this to be true. If a bird or animal cannot reason it cannot fear death, for it cannot anticipate death. Nature has conditioned it for its protection to be afraid of the unusual and the unknown but it does not know why it is afraid. This is why creatures take fright very easily, but just as easily carry on living normally once danger has passed. It follows then that a pheasant is no more frightened by a rough shooter's spaniel than a shepherd's collie. Nor is it more distressed by a beater flushing it by design than a picnicker by chance. In the course of a normal day it will receive a dozen frights – fright is a regular part of its life. Nor when it is flushed over a line of guns does it think with terror 'They are trying to shoot me'. It is simply one more experience from which instinct urges it to flee. In my view the pursuit of wild creatures does not cause them unusual mental anguish.

Suffering is another matter, for a wounded creature does suffer. How much it suffers I do not know. The impression I form is that, for a specific injury – say a broken leg – a wild creature suffers less than a human. But this may be because wild creatures have nothing to gain by making a fuss whereas humans have. But whatever the truth every shooting man should strive to avoid wounding a bird or animal, and if this happens he should make every effort to dispatch it as quickly as possible. In broad terms this means not taking shots beyond the limit of your skill or the range of your gun. It also means having a good dog to recover wounded creatures and Chapter 18 deals with this. No consideration, other than gun safety, should rank above the relief of suffering. For example if you wound a hare and it is dragging itself along, finish it off with the second barrel at once. It may only take seconds to recover and kill it, but this is no justification for not dispatching it instantly. Another rule is never to leave wounded game ungathered unless you have taken every possible step to recover it.

Having argued that distress is commonplace, and that suffering can be kept to a minimum, I am still exposed to the attack that we kill creatures which would otherwise be enjoying life. This argument ignores the realities of life outdoors, which is frequently uncomfortable, always cruel, and often attended by prolonged suffering. For example, in order to ensure the survival of a species, nature will provide for an abundance each breeding season which is often far higher than the natural food resources can sustain. Each winter sees the surplus starve and die, frequently taking a long time over the process during the hardest weather of the year. There are no drugs, anaesthetics or health services outdoors. Life is harsh and brutal. If I were a pheasant I would far rather be shot cleanly than die by whatever fate nature selected for me.

Of course an astute brain will pick flaws in the foregoing arguments and another keen brain can proffer further replies. The debate can, and will, continue for years. It is not my purpose to settle it, but simply to encourage beginners to the sport to think deeply about the various issues.

You should never kill lightly, nor without reason. Never shoot that which is neither eatable nor a pest, and never make a shot which you think may only wound. Learn to judge a day not upon the size of the bag, but upon the quality of the shots offered, the surroundings, and the company.

A final point of shooting ethics concerns sitting targets. At the highest level you will see Guns at a good-class driven shoot ignore pheasants which do not offer reasonably difficult targets. At the opposite extreme the fact that this book is written for beginners permits me to repeat the hairy old shooting joke about the Frenchman who was invited to a very formal English driven pheasant shoot. A cock pheasant scuttled out of the covert, and ran along in front of him. 'Don't shoot running pheasants', called out the host so the Frenchman waited until it stopped then shot it.

In general terms you should only shoot at a sitting target if it is a pest which requires destroying, or if the difficulty of approach warrants an easy kill when you arrive. An example of the first instance might be a crow on its nest, or a pigeon on spearing beans. The second instance is more arguable, and usually occurs in wildfowling. A typical example might be a handful of duck on the saltings where a long, dirty and difficult stalk could bring the fowler in range. Here he could argue, with justice in my view, that there was nothing unsporting in his killing a sitting duck with his first barrel. He would not, however, be entitled to 'brown' the party – that is fire at several bunched close together. This opportunity occurs not only at sitting but flying birds – grouse and partridge often give chances – and is unsporting, not least because it leads to wounded birds.

These, and many associated questions, will be paraded before your sporting conscience over the next few years. If you always place the welfare of the quarry uppermost you will arrive at the right answers.

Chapter 2

SHOOTING AND THE LAW

A somewhat bewildering variety of laws exist which regulate your ownership of a shotgun (or indeed any other firearm), where you use it, what you may shoot at, and when. All legislation is necessarily complex and that which touches upon shooting is certainly no exception. This chapter is simply my attempt to condense what would otherwise be a sizeable book into a few pages, and readers will be well advised to treat the results as opinions rather than facts, the more so as in some cases the penalties for infringement are severe.

The greatest temptation for the beginner with nowhere to shoot is to poach, and at first sight this can seem a very minor misdemeanour, partly because over the years writers have often glamorized the subject, and partly because the quarry is wild and it is difficult to credit ownership to any one man. The hard fact is that poaching is stealing, and if you pay a rent for shooting rights or spend time and money rearing pheasants only to suffer badly from poaching you will have no romantic illusions about the practice. I will deal with poaching at greater length, but to progress logically we must start with the right to own a gun. This is covered in detail by the Firearms Act of 1968, which lays down that any person who has in his possession, or purchases, or acquires a shotgun without holding a shotgun certificate will be guilty of an offence punishable on summary conviction by imprisonment for a term not exceeding six months, or a fine not exceeding £200, or both. The firearm may also be forfeited. This legislation was conceived not with a desire to restrict sportsmen, but in an effort to prevent shotguns being used in crime. At the time the sporting community opposed the proposals on the grounds that they would throw extra work on the police, cause inconvenience to shooting men, be a further restriction on individual liberty, and do nothing to prevent criminals using shotguns. Judging by results so far this view was correct, but whether the law was wise or not it exists and you must know it and comply.

The procedure is to visit you local police station; ask for and complete the necessary form, pay a fee of 75p and wait until the certificate is sent to you. You *must* be granted a certificate unless the Chief Constable has reason to believe that you cannot be permitted to possess a shotgun without danger to public safety or to the peace. There have been occasional difficulties encountered by applicants when certificates have been refused for inadequate reasons, and where the individuals have been members of WAGBI the Association has taken the matter up on their behalf. Apart from a few cases where the circumstances were impossible the Association has been successful, which is yet another reason for supporting WAGBI. A certificate can also be refused where the applicant has served a prison sentence, but the details of this aspect of the Act are lengthy, and I hope I am not being over-optimistic in hoping that so few readers will be effected that I am justified in omitting them.

At the time I write the possession of a certificate permits the holder to own or possess any number and types of shotgun. Whilst failure to carry the certificate with you when you have a gun is not an offence it is a sensible measure, for the police have power to seize the gun of anyone who cannot show a certificate. You will of course get it back when you produce the certificate but this is little consolation when you have missed a day's sport. You may not sell or transfer a gun to anyone other than a registered firearms dealer unless that person possesses a certificate. An important exemption for the beginner is that you may borrow a shotgun from the occupier of private premises and use it on those premises without a certificate, always provided that you are in his presence.

The position is that no one under the age of seventeen may purchase or hire a shotgun or ammunition, but they may be given either items unless they are under fifteen, when even this is an offence. If under the age of fifteen they cannot have with them an assembled shotgun unless under the supervision of someone over twenty-one, or unless the gun is in a securely fastened gun case such that it cannot be fired. In other words under the age of fifteen a boy may only be lent a gun, and can

31

only shoot under the care of someone over twenty-one. If he travels to or from the shoot without his mentor the gun must be in a case. He will still need a shotgun certificate unless he is exempted by one of the few special provisions.

Having acquired the right to possess a gun you are by no means free to go and fire it where, and at what, you want. The next requirement, at least for those who want to shoot game, is a Game Licence. This costs £6 for a full season, although a licence can be taken from the 1st August to 31st October for £4 and from the 1st November to the 31st July for the same amount. I quite frequently come across experienced shooting men who are unaware that a Game Licence is necessary to kill not only the accepted forms of game such as pheasant, partridge and grouse but snipe, woodcock and hares. In theory a Game Licence is necessary to kill even the humble rabbit, but in practise there are so many exemptions that you would be most unfortunate if you were prosecuted successfully. Game Licences are obtainable from any main Post Office, but not sub post offices. Whilst in the Post Office you may as well ensure that if you are a dog owner, and as a shooting man you should be, you hold a Dog Licence. This costs 37½p per year.

So far I have had little sympathy with the restrictions listed, for the shotgun certificate is a burden which does little or nothing for anybody's benefit and the Game Licence costs money which is in no way applied for the benefit of the sport. It is true that it helps to keep the country running, but no one has ever explained why I must buy a licence for my sport whereas my neighbours can play tennis, sail yachts, or strike inoffensive golf balls without doing so. The next barrier however, the Protection of Birds' Acts, 1954 to 1967, has my full support. Like most Acts it is long and involved, but so far as shooting is concerned the effect is to divide the birds into those that may never be shot, those that may be shot outside their close season, and those that may be shot at any time. The law in general and the four schedules dividing the birds into their special categories is comprehensively set out in an excellent little booklet entitled *Wild Birds and the Law*, published by the Royal Society for the Protection of Birds whose address is The Lodge, Sandy, Bedfordshire. There is little point in my detailing the law on every bird for there are few men who can

9 This young shot is removing his cartridge prior to crossing the fence.

10   A typical tunnel trap and another dead rat. Once set the trap needs covering with a very light layer of dry soil.

recognize every bird of these islands. The best practical rule for every shooting man is never to shoot any bird *unless he is quite certain that it is legitimate quarry.*

Birds which may be shot at any time include hooded and carrion crows, jays, magpies, rooks, both the black-backed gulls and wood pigeons; but they may only be shot by an authorized person as defined by the Act. Briefly this definition is that an authorized person is the owner or occupier of land or a person authorized by him. All the hawks and owls are protected at all times, some by special penalties.

The birds which may be shot outside the close season include not only the common quarries but coot, moorhen, bar-tailed godwit, curlew (other than stone curlew) and grey and golden plover. The close seasons are:

Grouse	12th August–10th December
Ptarmigan (Scotland only)	12th August–10th December
Black Game	20th August–10th December
Partridge	1st September–1st February
Pheasant	1st October–1st February
Capercaillie	1st October–31st January
Snipe	12th August–31st January

Wild Duck and Geese:
  In or over areas below high water mark of:

Ordinary spring tides	1st September–20th February
Elsewhere..	1st September–31st January

Woodcock:

In England and Wales	1st October–31st January
In Scotland	1st September–31st January

It is unlawful to shoot game on Christmas Day or Sundays. Duck and geese may be shot in most, but not all, counties in England on Sundays but not on Christmas Day. In most counties in Wales it is illegal to shoot ducks and geese on Sundays.

It is also illegal to sell dead wild geese. This is a relatively new law designed to stop the extensive shooting of geese on their inland feeding grounds for profit.

There is no close season for hares, but they may not be sold or offered for sale during the months of March to July inclusive.

Having carried out your legal obligations so far, and digested all the facts, you will be entitled to possess a gun and ammunition, to shoot game, and you will know what you may shoot and when you may shoot it. Which leaves the remaining question of where. With one important exception, which I will examine in detail shortly, there is nowhere that you can shoot without the consent of the owner or shooting tenant. Indeed if you enter private land without permission you are guilty not just of trespass but, under the 1968 Firearms Act, armed trespass, an offence which carries the penalty of not more than three months imprisonment or £100 fine, or both. As I wrote earlier, poaching is often treated lightly, principally by townsmen with no rural background, but the penalties that can be inflicted are severe. For both practical and moral reasons therefore you must resist the temptation to commit what, at first sight, may seem a trifling offence. You may have hunted an old cock pheasant along half a mile of hedges only for him to slip into a small copse just over the boundary. Temptation will tell you that he is morally yours, for is he not a resident on your ground who has temporarily crossed the boundary, and anyway it will only take a minute. But give way, shoot him, and get caught, and not only will you be charged with more offences than a common thief but you will deserve all you get.

The exception is with some foreshore shooting; and this is not so much a case of the public having a right to shoot as the owner not exercising his, or to be precise her, right to exclude them, for, unless there is evidence to the contrary, there is a presumption that the foreshore is owned by the Crown. For many years there was doubt as to precisely what ground constituted the foreshore, but legal battles have now established this. The rule is that the foreshore is bounded by the lines of the average of the ordinary tides recurring in the middle four day period between neap and spring tides. The landward boundary is the mean line reached by the flood of those tides, and the seaward boundary is the mean line of the ebb of these tides. There is no right to shoot on the foreshore whether it is owned privately or by the Crown, but in practise the Crown has never, or at least so far as I can

34

trace, attempted to prevent anyone so doing. For this reason over many years wildfowlers have grown accustomed to shooting over areas of foreshore and have, quite wrongly, grown to assume they shoot as of right. Until fairly recently a beginner could have found shooting in the form of wildfowling by visiting any of the numerous coastal areas where conditions encouraged a good population of wildfowl. But shooting pressures have now become so severe that many local wild-fowling clubs, either through WAGBI or on their own initiative, have negotiated foreshore leases either with the Crown or private owners. The practical effect of this, for the beginner, is that he can no longer drive to the coast and commence shooting but must assume that the foreshore is private until he discovers otherwise. Even if the shooting rights have not been privately leased a wildfowler is still liable for prosecution under the Firearms Act, 1968, for carrying a loaded shotgun onto the foreshore without permission. To counter this risk WAGBI has negotiated a form of authority which permits members with firearms to be present on Crown foreshore and open foreshore be-longing to the Duchy of Lancaster. This does not give WAGBI members the right to shoot, but it is a useful protection, and is yet another very good reason for shooting men to join the Association.

The law in Scotland is different, partly because the landward boundary is that reached by the highest of the spring tides, and secondly because the public enjoy a right to shoot on the foreshore. In all areas the creation of a sanctuary or reserve automatically cancels any shooting rights except those granted by the authorities administering the areas.

Although there is no legal obligation upon you to insure against any injury or damage you may cause with a gun this is a convenient chapter to deal with the subject. For a small premium each year you can insure both against third party claims for some tens of thousands of pounds, and against loss or damage to your gun, or guns. When you consider how easily a slip or a single careless action can seriously injure or kill another person, and the very substantial damages which could be awarded against you, I hope you will share my view that insurance is a very necessary precaution. It could well prevent you devoting part of your income for many years to paying off an award for damages and the victim of your error from being denied the money necessary for him to live a reasonable life. Most of the leading insurance companies will be willing to give you a quotation, and if you should have a young son who shoots you will be wise to have the cover extended to include him. It is not always realized that a parent can be liable for a child's negligence.

Chapter 3

GUNS AND CARTRIDGES

Readers of this book will range from the absolute novice thirsting for even the most elementary information to possibly the old hand who was given it for Christmas and is skipping through in the hope of finding a few new wrinkles. The more experienced will probably wish to skip the first part of this chapter, which explains in simple detail the names and functions of the various parts of a gun and cartridge.

This illustration on page 39 shows a conventional side by side double barrel gun. The various parts are numbered, and described below:

1. TOP RIB – A 'V' sectioned length of metal running between the two barrels to strengthen the joint. There is also a bottom rib serving the same function.
2. BARREL – A metal tube through which the shot pellets pass when the gun is fired.
3. FORWARD LUMP, HOOK OR BITE – A metal projection from the barrels which secures them to the action when the gun is closed.
4. REAR LUMP – Ditto.
5. TOP EXTENSION – An extension which strengthens the joint of the barrels and action. Usually only found on guns designed to fire heavier than average charges.
6. EXTRACTORS – which lift the cartridges clear of the barrels to facilitate removal when the gun is opened. With an ejector a fired cartridge is kicked out on opening.
7. TOP LEVER – A pivoted handle which when pushed sideways allows the gun to open. Guns have been made, but not recently, as side levers and under levers.
8. SAFETY CATCH – When on prevents the triggers being pulled in a box-lock action. One advantage of the type of mechanism known as a side-lock is that with the safety catch applied it is also impossible for a hammer to fall if the gun is badly jarred.

9. COMB – The portion of the stock illustrated.
10. STOCK – usually made of walnut.
11. HEEL OF STOCK
12. FORE-END PUSH BUTTON – for releasing the fore-end from the barrels.
13. FORE-END – of metal and wood construction. Limits the extent of opening, plays a part in cocking the hammers, and in ejectors contains the mechanism.
14. KNUCKLE OF ACTION – The fulcrum around which the barrels and action pivot.
15. ACTION – The working machinery of the gun. The illustration shows a box-lock. Side-lock actions can usually, but not always, be recognized by metal side plates extending into the stock above the triggers.
16. CROSS BOLT – engages in the top extension if fitted.
17. TRIGGER GUARD – Intended to shield the triggers to prevent accidental discharge.
18. FRONT TRIGGER
19. BACK TRIGGER
20. HAND OR SMALL OF GRIP
21. TOE OF STOCK

The purpose of the chequering on the hand of the stock is to prevent the hand slipping on discharge. It is a mistake to assume from this that the other hand should be placed on the chequering of the fore-end as, for most men, the correct position will be slightly forward. The metal faces of many parts of all but the cheapest guns are engraved, and in the best guns a very high standard of craftsmanship is involved. If the illustration could be viewed from above it would be seen that the stock was not in a continuous straight line with the barrels, but slightly bent to the right when viewed from the butt end. This assists the shooter to line up the eye with the barrels, and is known as 'cast-off'. The relationship of the stock to the barrels can be varied in this and other ways to ensure that the gun fits the individual owner, but obviously this is not possible with cheaper guns.

For the novice there must be a bewildering variety of combinations

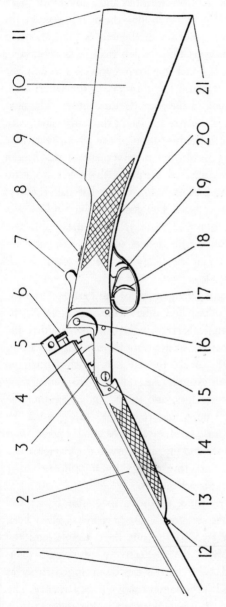

1. Top Rib
2. Barrel
3. Forward Lump, Hook or Bite
4. Rear Lump
5. Top Extension
6. Extractors
7. Top Lever

8. Safety Catch
9. Comb
10. Stock
11. Heel of Stock
12. Fore-end Push Button
13. Fore-end
14. Knuckle of Action

15. Action
16. Cross Bolt
17. Trigger Guard
18. Front Trigger
19. Back Trigger
20. Hand or Small of Grip
21. Toe of Stock

39

of weapons and sizes, but in fact practicalities and convention make the choice much simpler. We will consider the ideal weapon for the all-round shot in Chapter 5, but for the benefit of your shooting knowledge I will look at the variations which may be encountered. A brief look at history shows that the gun evolved through the smooth bore match lock in the fifteenth century, to the wheel lock, until the arrival of the flintlock in the seventeenth century. The next major step was the percussion muzzle loader in the early nineteenth century, and this endured until the invention of the pin fire cartridge some 25 years later made possible the development of the breech loader as we know it. For practical purposes there has been no major development in sporting guns design in the last half century, and I doubt there will be in the next. The design of the flintlock was responsible for the hammer gun (see Plate 3). Later the gunmakers concealed the hammers inside the action, so the first obvious distinction in the guns that you are likely to see in actual use is between hammer and hammer-less.

Next comes the number and arrangement of the barrels. Even the simplest gun of all, the single barrelled, offers wide variations. At the cheaper end we have the single barrel, single shot, with either the conventional 'drop down' method of inserting the cartridge or a bolt action. The next form of single barrel is the repeater, which is much the most commonly used gun in America. A repeater has a magazine which holds two or more cartridges, and the action of ejecting the spent cartridge, inserting the new, and re-cocking the gun can be performed either manually or automatically. Manual operation is performed by sliding the fore-end up and down the barrels. The automatics depend for their operating energy upon utilizing either part of the recoil force or the propellent gas.

Logically from single barrel guns we move to double barrel and there, for all practical purposes, we stop. There have occasionally been guns built with more than two barrels but their weight and the engineering problems involved have effectively prevented them coming into common use. Double barrels can be arranged either as 'over and under' or 'side by side', the names being self explanatory. The principal argument in favour of over and unders is that the narrower sighting plane, when compared with a side by side, makes for increased accuracy. Although over and unders are not unknown in conventional shoots, they are mainly favoured for the various forms of clay pigeon shooting.

Next we consider the size of bore, which simply means the diameter of the barrel. This is expressed by a number, e.g. 8 bore or 20 bore, and the figure means that this number of pure lead balls, each exactly fitting the bore, would weigh one pound. If you consider this for a moment you will see that the smaller the number the larger the bore, and here again the boundaries of practicability reduce a confusion of possibilities into a reasonable range. At the heavy weapon end I once collected from North Norfolk, on behalf of the Wildfowlers' Association, the double barrelled 4 bore used by Beris Harcourt Wood and bequeathed by him to WAGBI. The gun may now be seen at the Association H.Q. at Chester, but while it was in my possession I assembled it and had a few trial swings. (The illustration of a hammer gun, Plate 3, is of this weapon.) One could not but admire its massiveness and workmanship but for practical use it was a non-starter as the feature of balance, so desirable in a gun, was entirely absent. It could not be otherwise for the weight of the barrels alone precluded any such possibility. Impressive though its appearance might be it was inferior to a lighter well-balanced gun for 90 per cent of the chances likely to come the way of a wildfowler. And the same stricture, but to a lesser degree, applies to 8 and 10 bores. The 10 bore is taking a long time to die, but the introduction of British made extra heavy load 12 bore cartridges will hasten the end.

Among the lighter weapons the 28 bore is really only suitable for teaching a boy to shoot. 20 and 16 bores are used by boys, lady shots, and a limited number of men (an interesting point is that the majority of men shooting the smaller bores are excellent shots – generally speaking, the less proficient the shot the more he is tempted to buy the largest possible gun firing the greatest number of pellets).

We are left then with the 12 bore, and this size probably accounts for the vast majority of guns in use in Britain today. The shooting men of this country have not arrived at this conclusion by chance. The 12 bore has earned its popularity because experience has shown beyond question that it is the best compromise of weight and fire power. We will consider the question further in Chapter 5.

To state that the composition and functioning of the cartridge is simple is basically true, but this belittles the tremendous volume of research and development which has gone into making the modern cartridge so very consistent and reliable.

This illustration facing shows the make-up of a modern cartridge. Set in the centre of the base is the cap which, when it is set off by the striker, ignites the propellant powder stored around and above it. Cartridge powders are of nitro-cellulose compounds and have now been improved to the point where they are remarkably capable of resisting bad storage conditions. Notwithstanding this it is wise always to store your cartridges in dry conditions with moderate temperatures. Beyond the powder lies the wadding, a component whose importance is often underestimated. Its job is to seal the bore as it is thrust up the barrel by the tremendous pressure of the burning gases. The pellets are pushed before the wadding until they leave the barrel, when the larger bulk and lighter weight of the wadding slows it down in relation to the pellets. However, the wadding continues with considerable force. (A few weeks before writing this I shot a teal at dawn as it flighted into a rest pond in an overgrown osier-carr in North Norfolk. As it was quite close I was not surprised to find it appeared fairly heavily damaged when the spaniel retrieved it. In fact when I plucked it I found the entire wadding had entered the body just under one wing.) A badly fitting wadding allows propellant gases to creep around the side and reach the pellets, which can cause two problems. In mild cases the pressures created can cause havoc with the shot pattern, but where the leakage is severe the heat can actually fuse a number of pellets together, a process known as balling. This not only ruins the pattern, but also people and stock standing at what would normally be regarded as safe ranges.

The shot is not, as most people imagine, pure lead but is usually an alloy of lead, arsenic and antimony. The very best is plated with copper or nickel to prevent a process known as 'cold-welding' whereby groups of shot join together for all or part of their flight. It is highly unlikely that, when one considers all the other problems facing the

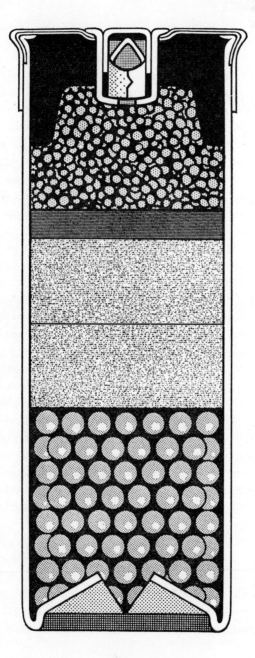

novice, increased results will justify the extra cost of chilled shot. Cartridges can, of course, be purchased with different shot sizes ranging from a few the size of ball bearings to dust shot which was once widely used for killing small birds for mounting without causing serious damage to the skins. In the same way that practical considerations eliminate the more extreme bore sizes so do they reduce the variety of shot sizes that the average shooting man need employ, and detailed advice on shot sizes is given in Chapter 5. It is dangerous to use cartridges of a greater length than the chamber of your gun.

A final word on cartridges. Time was that anyone who considered himself anyone in the shooting world had his cartridges especially hand loaded by one of the numerous gun makers scattered about the country, and these cartridges were considered superior to those mass produced. For all I know they may have been but I am sure that with present day labour problems and with improved techniques mass-produced cartridges offer better value for money. You will not be shooting for long before you discover that the cartridge market is dominated by one vast producer. Near monopolies have their disadvantages, but there are advantages too. In this case their supremacy has given them both the capital and the incentive to carry out massive research not only to improve the product but to reduce to a minimum inconsistencies in production. I hold no brief for the firm in question but I consider their policies and their pricing have always been fair and responsible and I am happy to pay credit. Do not be deceived if, after reading this, your local gun maker sells you a box of 'his' cartridges with his name on. The giant almost certainly manufactured them for him on the understanding that he placed a large enough order. If you like to buy 40,000 or so at once I suspect they will even put your name on.

Before leaving guns and cartridges there are a few miscellaneous points worth noting.

Always take down a gun slowly and carefully – many a scratch or dent has come from performing this operation hastily in confined quarters, such as the boot of a car. Never stand a gun against a wall, the side of a car, or other smooth surface on which it can easily slip and fall. The cost of taking even a modest dent from a barrel is alarming. Before the arrival of non-corrosive caps a gun had to be cleaned after each day's shooting. Now it is possible to leave it uncleaned for several days, but only if it has not become damp through rain or condensation. If it has then rust will form within hours and an immediate and thorough cleaning is essential. Even then it almost certainly has had some particles of damp creep into the working parts, and I always leave mine in the airing cupboard for several hours after cleaning. The non-corrosive caps of modern cartridges (beware the gift of very old cartridges given to you by a friend who found them in his attic) combined with several recently introduced proprietory gun oils have made cleaning a far easier job. A useful tip is to screw up two sheets from an absorbent toilet roll and push these through each barrel. They form a perfect size plug for a 12 bore, and take out 95 per cent of the fouling. With barrels in good condition a suitably sized patch on a jag will complete the job, but where discoloration is stubborn a phosphor-bronze brush should be used. The essential point about phosphor-bronze is that it is softer than the steel of the barrels. Finally the barrels need a light coating of oil. The top-flight clay shots usually wipe the oil clear, or fire a cartridge, before shooting seriously in the belief that the oil spoils the pattern. I would not know, but you will not see many of we rather more casual field shooters doing this. The remainder of the cleaning is mainly common sense – all moisture must go, and every visible metal part needs a light coat of oil. Places needing particular care are the valleys between the top and bottom ribs and the barrels, which hold dirt and damp, and the breech face which sometimes becomes pitted through the action of leakages of hot propellant gases. The stock will benefit from an occasional drop of artists' quality linseed oil, but too much will produce a gum-like coating. Mud should be gently wiped from the stock with a soft, damp cloth and brushed from the crevices in the chequering with a tooth-brush and warm water. Never clean the chequering with a hard instrument. And never, never attempt to be your own gunsmith – the craft calls for years of apprenticeship and special tools. At the least you may do expensive damage, and you could easily render the gun dangerous. As the doctor said 'clean your ears out with your elbows', or in other words – leave things alone.

'Proofing', an important matter in the world of guns, is dealt with in Chapter 5.

Chapter 4

BASIC BALLISTICS

It is not difficult to comprehend the action of the gun and cartridge. The cap, ignited by the blow of the hammer, sets fire to the powder. The powder literally burns and does not explode or detonate as does a military explosive such as T.N.T. But the rate of burning is incredibly fast, and the gases produced occupy a volume many times greater than the powder. The pressure forces the wadding against the pellets which in turn are forced against the crimp or roll–top closure of the cartridge. This bursts open, the wadding and the pellets shoot up and out of the barrel and the whole of this simple operation is completed. Except that it is not simple. It is, in fact, highly complex. Consider the problems of producing a cap which can withstand being rough handled with perfect safety in railway wagons, yet fire every time when given a not over violent blow by the striker. Or a powder whose rate of burning is so consistent that thousands upon thousands of cartridges discharge their pellets at practically the same muzzle velocity.

Fortunately those problems rest squarely on the shoulders of the cartridge manufacturers, and their penalty for failing to continue to solve them is that we will change to another brand. There are, how-ever, some aspects of the ballistical behaviour of the gun and cartridge which concern us very deeply for they influence our choice of both, and how we use them.

When the pellets leave the muzzle of a 12 bore they are tightly packed in a cylindrical shape and rather less than an inch in diameter. This shape immediately begins to break up and each pellet follows its own individual flight path. This divergence is caused by minute variations in weight, shape, air pressures, and certain other reasons, none of them of any great significance but each sufficient to cause small differences. If at any point in the flight of the charge a large card were interposed, each pellet would punch a hole, and the resultant picture of the distribution of the charge would be called the pattern. This is, in fact, the recognized system of calculating the performance of a gun and cartridge. The standard practice is to fire a shot from a previously fired gun at a sheet of paper not less than four feet square, and at a carefully measured range of 40 yards. A 30-inch diameter circle is then drawn from the apparent centre of the pattern, and the number of pellets in the circle counted. This is repeated five times and the average of the pellet counts taken. This figure can then be expressed as a percentage of the known pellet load in the brand of cartridge. As an aside let me stress that if the gun is to kill consistently it is important that it shall not only throw the required number of pellets into the circle but distribute them evenly. If pellets are tightly clustered in some areas but very sparse in others it becomes quite possible to aim true yet fail to strike the quarry. Obviously this risk is higher with a small quarry such as a snipe than with a cock pheasant.

It would be wrong to assume that the object is to throw the highest possible percentage of pellets into the magic 30-inch circle. This is merely a measuring device to assist in regulating the barrels of a gun to perform as we wish them to for our particular form of shooting. If at the instant at which the shot charge reaches the target it is still tightly packed the chances of missing will be high. Conversely if the pellets have spread very widely there is a danger that the pattern will contain open areas through which the quarry will escape. Obviously it is not possible to arrange matters so that the quarry is always shot at the same range, so the regulation of the barrels must depend on the type of shooting the individual does. A man who principally shoots fast moving driven game at close ranges would have barrels designed to allow the shot to spread quickly, whereas a gun designed for wildfowling, where much of the shooting is done at the longer ranges, would keep the charge together for as far as possible. Regulating or controlling the spread of the pellets is a considerable part of the gunsmith's art, and this is achieved by giving the barrels choke.

Choke is simply a constriction; a reduction of the diameter of a barrel at the muzzle. This is not, of course, an abrupt stepping down of the diameter but a very gradual reduction. The effect is to give those pellets on the outside an inward impetus so that the charge flies more closely and spreads less. To give practical examples a true cylinder barrel, that is one with no choke whatsoever, would put about 40 per cent of its pellets into the 30-inch circle at 40 yards. A full choke barrel, that is one choked so far as is practicable, would achieve about 70 per cent. So you see the difference is very considerable, and allows us a wide choice as to how we wish our guns to perform.

The tendency with beginners is to buy heavily choked guns in the belief that the intense concentration of pellets will have a high killing power and greater range. So they will, but a considerably higher degree of skill will be called for in order to hit the target. Shooting is difficult, and there is no point in making it unnecessarily harder. The more experienced a shooting man the more likely he will be to have his gun fairly lightly choked. In so doing he will have reduced his chances of bringing off occasional impressive long range kills, but if he is a sportsman he will not attempt such shots, choke or no choke. Far too many of these end in a wounded bird or animal. There are several ways of expressing the degree of choke but probably the most common names six stages: true cylinder, improved cylinder, quarter choke, half choke, three-quarters choke and full choke. The following table, from the *Eley Shooters' Year Book*, shows the effect of the various degrees of choke.

Percentage of total pellets in 30-inch circle

Boring of gun	Range in yards						
	30	35	40	45	50	55	60
True cylinder	60	49	40	33	27	22	18
Improved cylinder	72	60	50	41	33	27	22
Quarter choke	77	65	55	46	38	30	25
Half choke	83	71	60	50	41	33	27
Three-quarter choke	91	77	65	55	46	37	30
Full choke	100	84	70	59	49	40	32

There is nothing better than an argument on chokes and patterns to pass the time away when several shooting men are driven to shelter by

11   A rearing field in June with the newly hatched pheasant chicks and their broody hens being transferred to the rearing pens.

12　Keepers feed their pheasant coverts daily and in hard weather many other birds benefit

rain, and the novice listening to the wide differences of opinion between the experts would wonder what hope he had of reaching a conclusion. Personally I find that the quarry, and the conditions under which we pursue them, vary so widely that there is no perfect answer. However I am quite certain that many people have guns which are choked too tightly for the owners' ability. Logically one may as well benefit by the experience of others, and I am sure that a census of the barrel chokings of the above average shots of Britain would show a majority favouring improved cylinder for the right barrel and half or three-quarter choke for the left. For a man who expected to do a preponderance of wildfowling, or moorland rough shooting, where it is difficult to get near the quarry, it might be wise to have the right barrel quarter choke and the left full. Some men who only shoot driven game, where range is rarely a factor but rapid shooting is, have both barrels bored improved cylinder.

If, in spite of these comments, you are keen to have a heavily choked gun then by all means buy one; it is far cheaper to remove choke from barrels than put it in. But if you find your marksmanship fails to improve as you feel it should, the answer may well be in the gun rather than you.

Given all this basic information we can now consider some other ballistical aspects. A question you must resolve for yourself is the size of shot to fire. There is a bewildering choice.

As you will appreciate a particular variety of cartridge is designed for a specific weight of shot and you can choose between a large number of small pellets or a small number of large pellets, or various graduations in between. Beginners often select the larger pellets in the belief that these will do more harm, which is perfectly correct except that before pellets can do harm they have to hit the target and a few large pellets are less likely to do this than a great many small ones. It is a fact, and one worth keeping firmly in mind, that pattern fails before penetration. This means that the pattern develops what we will call escape holes before the individual pellets, unless they are very small, have lost their power to penetrate fur and feather plus any major organ or bone they meet. Remember it is not sufficient just to hit the target – you must hit it in a vital place, and preferably several, if it is to be

4

cleanly killed. Furthermore if you remove the feathers and non-vital materials from, for example, a pheasant, you will see how small the actual target really is.

There is a lot of nonsense talked about shot sizes by people who have never really considered the subject. Let us assess it logically. To give ourselves the best chance we need the closest possible pattern, but it must be of shot sufficiently heavy to do the job when it gets there. In other words we want the smallest size shot that carries sufficient punch. That mine of information, *The Shooters' Year Book*, gives a table of the number of pellets which have to strike different creatures, at minimum striking velocities, in order to achieve a clean kill. If we ignore the geese, which are rare targets, and the small birds on the assumption that what kills the big ones will kill the small, and consult the table for medium size birds we are told that a minimum of three pellets, each with a striking energy of 0·85 foot lb, are necessary to kill. The table instances a medium bird as a grouse, and as I suspect a cock pheasant or a mallard needs a little more killing let us raise the striking energy figure to 1 foot lb. I believe 40 to 45 yards is the maximum range at which you should normally shoot – certainly 50 yards. Beyond that, few men have the necessary degree of skill and it becomes a most unsporting matter of potting vaguely away and hoping.

Given these facts the critical question becomes – what is the smallest size of shot which has a striking energy of not less than 1 foot lb at 50 yards? The answer is No. 6 which has a striking energy of exactly 1 lb.

Once I spent a lot of time bothering about shot sizes, but now I buy No. 6's and use them at everything, with the single exception of wildfowling trips for geese when I use No. 1's. If the manufacturers suddenly stopped producing No. 6's (which is unlikely as they must represent the majority of their sales) and I had to change I would move to the smaller No. 7 rather than a larger pellet. (For those who do not appreciate the Irishness of it, as the number of the shot goes up the size goes down.)

You may wonder why one's chances cannot be improved by making a longer cartridge to take more pellets. This practice is common, particularly in America where they seem to spend more time devising ever larger cartridge loads than actually shooting, but there are snags. The relationship between the standard gun and cartridge is fairly delicate and even to increase the number of pellets by a modest few per cent produces an appreciable increase in recoil (the recoil increases as the weight of charge increases unless the weight of the gun is also increased). After firing a few shots this increased recoil could possibly have a more detrimental effect on one's marksmanship than the good done by the extra pellets (which only help on the long range shots anyway). Additionally, constantly firing the heavy charge will not be good for the gun. You can resolve this by buying a heavier gun, classed as a magnum, designed for the really heavy load cartridges. But this will be much heavier to carry, harder to shoot with because of its weight, and when you take the not so infrequent close shots there will be no need to pluck the bird – the shot will have done that for you.

As a matter of interest, in the standard 12 bore cartridge loaded with $1\frac{1}{16}$ oz shot there are 131 No. 4 pellets, 287 No. 6 pellets, and 478 No. 8 pellets. Therefore the man who swears by No. 4's is firing nearly 100 less pellets than the No. 6 adherent – consider how much more quickly escape holes must develop in the pattern.

The question of recoil is most important when considering a gun for a younger person, for his early failures at correct mounting will exaggerate the normal shock. The kick of a 12 bore is sufficient for most men, and a boy using this size of gun can well develop a habit of flinching as he pulls the trigger. I would unhesitatingly recommend a 20 bore, which is light enough for a boy to handle yet throws enough charge for most normal shooting. My eldest son has used one since he was twelve, with good results.

There have been a goodly number of books written on the technical aspects of guns and cartridges, but if you want to learn more I recommend *Shotguns and Cartridges* by Gough Thomas, published by A & C Black Ltd., at £1·50. Another very useful book by the same author is *Gough Thomas's Gun Book* at £2·40. Gough Thomas not only knows his subject extremely well, but he can put what are really rather dull facts across in an exceptionally clear and interesting fashion.

Chapter 5

SELECTING A GUN

You will not have to be a very astute reader to have gathered from my comments in Chapter 3 that I have little time for the extremes in gun sizes. A frequent characteristic of newcomers to the sport is to change weapons regularly, always convinced that the new purchase is going to do great things for their marksmanship. Time brings wisdom, and they gradually learn that the only thing that really matters is to point the barrels in the right direction when they pull the trigger. The most important factor in achieving this ideal is not the gun or the cartridge but themselves. Or put another way, a good shot will perform well with almost any gun, but no permutation of barrels, bores, or cartridge loads will make a marksman of a duffer. One of the best pigeon shots I know, a Cambridgeshire man, uses his grandfather's old hammer 12 bore, the muzzles of which will soon be dangerously thin.

This is not to say that there is no point in deliberating carefully over the gun you buy – there is; but first you must establish very clearly in your mind the qualities you are seeking, and these will be determined by the forms of shooting you intend to follow. Looking at fundamentals our sport is concerned with shooting moving objects, and it follows that a gun must be well balanced and as light as possible. A heavy gun is acceptable for distant targets following a steady path, but it is an unlucky man whose sport is confined to one form of target. As an example, I once bought a double barrel 10 bore for wildfowling, fondly thinking I would cope with those mallard which had been sneaking past at extreme range for my 12 bore. Cope it did, but humping the brute over the marshes took a lot of the pleasure away, and eventually an evening came which led to its sale. I had decided to take evening flight on a small 'fleet', as inland stretches of water are called in Kent, where I was shooting. I had no great hopes, but, as the light went, a most wonderful flight of teal developed. Birds were dropping in all round me but their small size and the bad light meant snap shooting. With the big heavy 10 bore I might as well have tried to swat them with a fence post. A good rule to remember all your shooting life is: A GUN NEEDS TO BE AS LIGHT AS POSSIBLE, BUT CAPABLE OF PROJECTING COMFORTABLY A SUFFICIENTLY HEAVY CHARGE OF SHOT.

If you stick to this principle in selecting a gun you will not go far wrong. In fact the solution for the novice is even easier, for this problem has been posed and solved many, many times and my task is simply to persuade you to accept the lessons of experience. Generation after generation of shooting men have gone through their early experimental phase and eventually concluded that a double barrelled, side by side, 12 bore, firing a standard load cartridge, is the ideal.

I could have said this in the first paragraph but I wished to stress the position logically as there is some strange force which lures newcomers into resisting tradition and sallying forth, armed with paper theories, to buy something different. Not unnaturally the gun makers and salesmen are not renowned for talking down these theories. My own dealer, with whom I would hastily add I remain on the best of terms, cheerfully helped me plunge my way through a wide range of guns before I eventually bought a pair of matched 12 bores with which I expect to shoot with complete contentment for the rest of my life. I suppose the truth is that if you admit the gun is not at fault then the only other culprit must be yourself.

The statistical reasons why the 12 bore has received almost universal acceptance among men are such that it conforms well with the principle I set out earlier in this chapter. In other words it is the lightest gun capable of comfortably projecting a sufficiently heavy charge of shot. To elaborate slightly let us consider a gun using No. 6 shot, which I showed in the previous chapter is sufficiently heavy for all normal use. The need is for a gun with a bore of such a diameter that it can hold and fire the quantity of shot necessary to give an adequate pattern density at 50 yards, which is the range I have suggested as the maximum. The size of a 12 bore is such that it adequately answers this need; anything smaller does not, and anything bigger is unnecessarily heavy.

Some readers may be tempted to 16 or 20 bores with the idea of enjoying their lightness over a 12 bore and making up the discrepancy in the weight of shot by using a heavy load cartridge. However, as I explained in the previous chapter, this practice carries the drawbacks of increased recoil and decreased gun life. A further snag is that a long thin column of shot, as fired from a smaller bore, will give an inferior pattern to a short fat column of shot, of similar weight, fired from a 12 bore. For a boy, lady, or man in poor health a 16 or 20 bore is ideal, but I see no reason for a man to handicap himself artificially. On many occasions, for example, knocking down wood pigeons coming into decoys at twenty yards, the smaller bores will do, but inevitably the time comes when more weight of shot is needed. The criticism that at close quarters the 12 bore is sometimes too powerful is answered by the availability of light load 12 bore cartridges.

I hope you will find these views fairly conclusive but equally if you really want to experiment with different weapons then I would hate to deter you. There is a great deal of fun to be had from so doing. The first pinkfoot I shot was under the moon on The Wash, and the excitement and romance would have been slightly less had I not killed it with a beautiful old hammer 10 bore by Tolley. My companion at the time still tells the story of hearing my voice, sharp with tension, float across the marsh, 'Clive – I've shot a goose – and I can't find it!' I did, which is hardly surprising for I intended to strain the entire Wash through my bare fingers before I gave up. It was the same companion who would wait for geese at dawn with a very long single barrel 8 bore, and a spare cartridge clenched between his teeth.

How then do you go about buying a gun? Assuming you have your shotgun certificate you can buy either from a dealer or a private individual. The advantage of a dealer who has a well-established business is that he is far more concerned with maintaining his reputation than catching you for a tenner or so. He will, and quite rightly, make a sensible profit margin on the deal but unless you know gun values which, contrary to what one might think by listening to them, few people do, it is only by buying from a dealer that you can be sure of value for money. Another good reason for buying from the trade is concerned with the laws of Proof. To go into detail on this subject would take some pages and not greatly advance your practical knowledge, so I will briefly define the Proof laws as a set of rules designed to prevent the sale of shotguns in an unsafe condition. The two bodies legally appointed to apply the laws are the Worshipful Company of the Gunmakers of the City of London and the Guardians of the Birmingham Proof House, and on manufacture in this country all guns have to be submitted to one of these bodies for proving. The proving arrangements for most foreign countries are acceptable here, and the majority of the guns imported do not have to be re-proved on arrival. Proof involves an examination of the gun generally, but the most stringent tests are applied to the barrels, as the greatest danger in using a gun is a burst barrel. This can come either through a flaw in the metal or insufficient thickness to give the necessary strength. The major test is to fire, by remote control, a cartridge which produces considerably more pressure than any normal cartridge. After a gun has passed the tests the flats of the barrels are stamped with a proof mark which will vary according to the proof house but will now always include the letters NP (standing for nitro proof). It can be taken for granted that a new gun is proved, but a secondhand gun may well be out of proof. The two main reasons for this both relate to barrel wall thicknesses having fallen below the safe minimum. One cause is neglect which leads to pitting in the bores which is then machined out. The other, which is much rarer, is just sheer hard use whereby the frequent passage of shot, wadding, and hot gases simply wears the barrels thin. An additional danger with a really old gun is that, nitro powders being a comparatively recent invention, it has only been proved for black powder. As nitro powders are more powerful there is a serious danger of a burst if standard cartridges are used.

In other words if you buy a new gun there is no danger, but the proof marks on a secondhand gun are no guarantee. This is where the advantage of buying from a dealer occurs. It is illegal to sell a gun out of Proof, and a dealer has not only the instruments and the experience to check the condition of the barrels but a very strong incentive to do so. His reputation is at stake, whereas the private individual is far less concerned. However, I would not turn you entirely against a private deal. You are unlikely to pay much too much with a dealer but you are even more unlikely to pay much too little. Privately you can get caught but you can sometimes do very well. The best advice is not to buy a gun privately without first submitting it to a professional for an opinion.

There is a further reason for buying from a dealer – you need a gun that fits. Shortly I deal with the question of marksmanship, and it is a pre-requisite that your gun is the right size for you. This means the right size in several different ways, and the variations are intended to allow you to mount the gun smoothly, and then find it in the position to aim and fire instantly. For example, when the butt is bedded smoothly in the right shoulder the right eye should be looking straight down the centre of the rib. The consequences in marksmanship of having to mount the gun and then roll the head to left or right to line up the eye can be imagined. Few private individuals will have the experience to tell you whether a gun fits, and as they will have only one weapon to sell they would not apply it if they had. The dealer, for the reasons I have explained earlier, will be anxious to sell you a suitable gun.

So far I have carefully referred to buying a gun that fits, but there is a higher, indeed at todays prices one might almost write, celestial, stage where one orders a gun, or guns, to be built that are fitted. Many older writers on shooting obviously regarded the possession of a fitted gun, or guns, as an essential first step in marksmanship, and to this day it is common to read this argument. I must confess it does read well but for all but a lucky minority it is financially impossible. Nor do I agree that a fitted gun is essential for good shooting. If a man has a gun that fits reasonably well he can quickly learn to adapt himself to any really minor variations.

How much should one pay? The only answer is as much as you reasonably can. A new gun can cost anywhere between £50 and £2,000, and both will take the same cartridge and kill almost as well. But whereas the one will be a joy to hold and use the other will feel a crude tool, and the better gun, being by far the better balanced and having the sweeter mechanical action, will permit better marksmanship. Equally obviously the better a gun the less the chance of it failing mechanically, and also the more its value will appreciate with time. If

13 Replacing a polecat ferret in its sack before moving on to another burrow.

▲14 Contrary to popular belief, ferrets,
     if frequently handled from birth,
     are quite safe with humans.

▼15 An English partridge in hard
     weather.

▲16   Hare at speed. Notice the great travel and length of the rear legs.

▼17   Cock pheasant on ice. When the ground is frozen pheasants are denied many of their food sources.

▲18 Even sparse cover is better than nothing. Breaking up the usual human silhouette is a great help.

▼19 Hen pheasants bursting from the cover of a potato clamp.

you can afford £200 then you can, at least as I write, buy a good new English gun. £75 will buy a perfectly serviceable secondhand one and, given time and care, £25 will find a gun which although crude would be safe. It is important not to bother overmuch about the value of your gun. Nothing could be more false than to believe that because you are armed with a cheap firearm you can never be more than a second-rate shot.

Once, on the Isle of Skye, I slipped whilst stalking a hoodie crow over rocks by a loch side and badly dented my gun barrels. Reluctantly I borrowed the keeper's gun, a cheap pre-war Continental piece in bad condition with the barrels badly pitted, and the top lever spring broken. I tied a rubber band from the trigger guard to the top lever, and shot with it for the rest of my stay. My percentage of kills to cartridges remained the same, and I seriously doubt I would have bagged any-thing extra with my own gun.

There is much to be said for buying a secondhand gun for unlike cars, cameras, and other complex mechanical devices, it is fairly easy for an expert to examine a gun and predict its remaining life. Ten years ago I would have urged you to buy an English gun, either new or secondhand, in preference to foreign, but the standard of some, I stress some, foreign guns has improved considerably. Some rubbish comes from abroad but the better makes are good value.

For several reasons, but more particularly price, you may be tempted to buy a repeater. I would urge you not to do so. The considerations which lead me to this plea are part practical, and we will take these first. The design characteristics of all repeaters are such that their balance is inferior to conventional, by which I mean side by side, guns. Conventional guns are safer as it is simpler to see that the breeches are empty, and additionally by leaving the gun 'broken' one's companions can be shown the fact in a subtle fashion. Repeaters are more prone to malfunctions. Conventional guns have the great advantage that the sportsman can choose instantly between the chokes of his two barrels – the repeater owner is limited to one choke only. If the repeater has provision for only two cartridges its fire power is no better than that of a conventional gun, and if it has provision for more then you should on no account use it. This may seem a remarkable statement to the novice who feels the basic object of the exercise is to kill something and the more shots the greater the chance. This philosophy is quite wrong, and if by the end of this book you still cannot understand my abhorrence to multi-shot repeaters then I have made a bad job of writing it. One goes shooting for many different reasons which range from observing the pattern of hoar frost on a twig to getting a brace of pheasants for your doctor. One does not go shooting to blaze as many as five cartridges at some poor beast. Ideally we would allow ourselves one shot only, but because we are human and weak with it I suppose two is reasonable. But if you cannot hit it with two then let it go. Five shot repeaters are for murderers not sportsmen. There is a school of thought that accepts the principle but argues that where, for example, a large party of pigeons or duck comes over five shots can be fired at separate birds. In some cases, for example where pigeons are hitting a crop hard, I accept this, but in general few species are so plentiful that a man should attempt to kill five at one encounter. It is all very well to argue that the extra magazine capacity is used only on justifiable occasions, but with five in the magazine the temptations to twitch the trigger for a third at a sly old January cock must be very strong.

For these reasons, and because it resembles a military weapon, and because convention decrees that it is unacceptable, the repeater is virtually never seen at a formal shoot. At this stage of your sporting career your future participation in formal shoots may seem too distant to consider, but it does seem good sense to buy at the beginning a gun which will be acceptable in any company.

Chapter 6

SAFETY

THE FIRST PRIORITY

I once lived near a small family of father, mother and a twenty-year-old son. They were a most pleasant group, and normal in every way except that the boy had lost his right leg. His father had accidentally blown it off with a shotgun. Can you imagine not only the physical pain but the permanent mental agony of both the boy, who would be always denied the pleasure of so many physical activities, and the father, who realized how much his error had cost his own son.

I am sorry to start this chapter on such a gruesome note but it is essential that every shooting man fully realizes just how dangerous a gun is. For several years I acted as captain to a syndicate on a Yorkshire grouse moor, and I made sure that the regular Guns were safe shots. However, two of the Guns were taken by our landlords who filled them with a variety of businessmen they wished to please, and, while all our guests were pleasant, we saw some remarkable ideas on gun safety. These varied from the Frenchman who stepped into his butt and pulled on a pair of shot-proof goggles, to the experienced Gun who peppered the occupants of the next butt but one and flatly denied firing anywhere near them. I mention this later incident because it is a mistake for the beginner to go out with an experienced Gun and assume that what he sees is safe gun handling. Unlike car driving there is no test to pass, and a man can be an unsafe shot all his life.

If you have any doubts about the killing potential of a gun take a piece of soft wood $\frac{3}{4}$-inch thick (which has much the same resistance as the human skull) and fire at it from two yards. No further demonstration will be necessary.

Over the years a code of rules for gun safety has been built up, and the basis of these rules is the fact that if every man pointed his gun only at that which he sought to kill, and then pulled the trigger only if absolutely positive that there was nothing else in the path of the shot, then there would be no shooting accidents. From this stems the main rule: never point your gun at anything other than the earth or the sky unless you mean to kill it. This sounds simple enough, but its application under field conditions is difficult. There are two situations, firstly when you are simply carrying or holding the gun and secondly the act of shooting. To assist with the first convention has decreed two basic positions for carrying the gun; either over the arm with the trigger guard resting on the forearm and the barrels pointing at the ground, or with the barrels resting on the shoulder and pointing at the sky with the hand grasping the small of the stock and the trigger guard up (with the guard down the angle of the barrels drops sharply). The over-the-arm position can be somewhat dangerous in icy or muddy conditions for the gun sits loosely and a slip can cause it to fly about wildly. These two positions are good when relaxed, but when action is imminent a more ready position is necessary. When stationary, and this applies equally to the wildfowler kneeling in a creek or a Gun standing by a peg waiting for driven pheasants, the stock can be raised and gripped between the biceps and the body, and the barrels pointed skywards at about 45 degrees. For the moving rough shooter the two hands can again hold the gun in a ready position but the barrels must either point down into the ground or up to the sky. These angles of the barrels are not the best for mounting the gun, but they are safest. The most dangerous attitude, and one seen all too frequently, is the man who holds the gun parallel with the ground. Although the stationary driven game man may start by pointing the barrels at right angles to the line, the natural tendency is for the gun to creep round to lie across his chest and thereby point at his neighbour. Even if it does not, as the beaters approach it becomes equally menacing to them. This angle is even worse with the rough shooter out with companions, for every time the right foot goes forward the barrels must move towards any companion on his left.

The second situation of the main rule, the act of shooting, means never shooting where you cannot see, or perhaps to make it a little clearer, never shooting where you cannot see everything. The danger here is the man who shoots at a rabbit as it disappears into a hedge, the partridge as it tops a straw stack, or the woodcock as it flits through the wood. Hours before writing this I watched a very experienced sportsman take a quick snap at a hen pheasant as it flashed down a hedge. The charge passed through, and narrowly missed another Gun who had, unbeknown to the first, left his peg. The history of shooting tragedies is full of similar accidents which have been committed by both novices and experienced Guns. Any shot which is fired into a wood or a hedge is unsafe unless fired upwards at such an angle that it cannot strike a man, and even then unless the leaves have fallen there is the one in a million chance of hitting an adventurous child.

It is even more potentially fatal to shoot at movement. A typical situation would be the man ferreting rabbits who shoots at a movement in the grass near to the burrow. It is almost certainly a rabbit but it might be a small dog. I know personally of a fatal accident to a human which occurred in recent years in this way.

Whenever you climb a gate (which, incidentally, you should never do unless it cannot be opened, and only then close to the hinges), jump a stream, cross a fence or crawl through a hedge, *always* unload your gun. Never load your gun before you need to, and unload it immediately shooting ceases. Never give, or accept, an unbroken gun, which should, of course, be empty. When standing in a group or meeting someone in the field always break your gun. There is some controversy over this, usually from members of more formal shoots where it would be unthinkable not to unload a gun between drives. They contend that a shoot which requires guns to be broken is casting aspersions on the sanity of the members, and that additionally it is mechanically bad for a gun to be carried about in the relatively weak open position. My own view is simple and strong – the best of us make mistakes, and if a gun is open everyone, the owner included, is certain it is empty. Wherever I have had the responsibility for a shoot I have always asked that guns should be broken. In this I may have offended some, but no-one was ever shot. It is obvious that one should never put down a loaded gun, whether it is leaned against a hedge or placed on a car seat. An extension of this precaution is to keep guns and cartridges in separate places and locked. This is doubly necessary when there are children in the house.

The distance shot carries depends upon the size and the angle of the gun to the ground on discharge. It is wise to assume that it is dangerous up to 400 yards or so for shot not larger than No. 4. Never, therefore, fire towards people, stock, buildings, or any other sensitive target at less than this. In practice the shot will not carry this far unless pointed at the optimum angle, and even if it does the force of impact will be small. However, it is sensible to avoid all risk. A pellet in the eye does not need much force to do damage, and a lorry driver startled by the rattle of shot on the windscreen, to give an example, could cause a major accident. Never shoot near horses with riders.

Guns with badly neglected barrels or well maintained guns with the barrels blocked with mud or snow can burst on firing. It is sensible to check the barrels after a fall. Also check after firing a cartridge that sounds or feels abnormal. I recently had a cartridge from a well-known maker where the cap failed to ignite the powder which was left dotted in an unburnt state along the length of the barrel. The wad had been expelled but had it remained as a blockage in the barrel the next shot could have caused a burst.

It is foolish for two beginners to shoot together – shoot with an experienced man or shoot alone. Once, rough shooting in Scotland, a fellow guest at the hotel asked if he and his fourteen-year-old son could join me. He was, he assured me, very experienced, and had brought his son up properly. The falseness of this claim was demonstrated in the first few yards when they both climbed through a barbed wire fence with loaded guns. Eventually the son wounded a grouse, and then set about killing it by grasping his gun by the barrel and clubbing the bird to death. Fortunately for him it was a single barrel, for had it been a double the jarring could easily have fired the second barrel into his body. Ignoring the safety factor it was also a certain way to damage the gun, and an inhuman manner of dispatching game. His father was considerably older than I, and I said nothing, but it was a cowardly mistake and for the sake of them both I should have read the riot act.

For the experienced shot the foregoing has been written so often that it is boring, and even for the beginner it is all basic common sense. The real danger comes, however, in the excitement of shooting. It is not difficult to avoid pointing the gun in the wrong places when standing or walking, but when every eye or nerve is concentrated on the quarry it is all too easy. The most common crime committed by experienced shots at formal shoots is to swing the gun through the line of Guns whilst following the target. If the gun is discharged at the wrong moment an accident follows automatically. The only solution is to control one's actions with a cast iron will. *If you are not certain the shot is safe then do not pull the trigger.* Novices kill people because they commit fundamental errors. Experienced Guns kill because they relax their normal safety standards for a fraction of a second. After the basic rules are observed the major risk for the beginner is the rash shot, taken because he is so keen to bag the quarry. This temptation is all the greater with young people, who are usually even more keen to score than the mature adult.

Moving beyond the novice and considering safe and experienced Guns it is a fact that their safety margins are not constant but vary from day to day, and even hourly. A blazing row the previous day with a business partner, lack of sleep, or an extra drink at lunch can all lead a man to take a chancy shot. So can a succession of misses, with an increasingly irritated Gun thinking more of killing the next one than safety. It is a wise man who recognizes these pressures, and spots them in himself. There are some men who are temperamentally unsafe. They may have untidy minds and be forever unsure whether their gun is loaded or not, or whether the keeper has left a stop in the corner of the wood. There are others who simply cannot doubt their infallibility and consistently shoot too close to others, while assuring them afterwards that there was nothing to worry about. If they have been shooting for a long time nothing you say will cure them – you will only offend. The sight of blood will bring them to their senses, but it is then too late – the more so if it is your blood.

Always remember that the moment you pick up a gun you are just one foolish action and an instant of time away from killing somebody. There is no quarry and no circumstances that justify taking even the smallest risk.

Chapter 7

MARKSMANSHIP

Marksmanship is the art of hitting the target. Many people who take up shooting have previously had experience with rifles, and it is important to appreciate that the two forms of technique are very different. Rifle shooting is a science performed slowly and calculatingly – shotgun shooting is an art, depending to a considerable degree on instinct and conditioned reflexes. Some men are born good shots with a natural sense of timing, others are not, but whatever your level of inherited ability it can be enhanced by practice and observing the correct techniques. There is no absolutely perfect technique for shooting any more than there is only one correct golf swing. Each individual will prefer minor variations, but there are some basic rules which although experienced men can ignore and still shoot well, they would most certainly perform better if they observed them.

We must consider three separate acts in the process of firing a gun: raising it to the firing position, the firing position, and the act of firing. It is pointless to consider how best to raise, or to use the correct term – mount – the gun until we know the position to which to raise it, so I will detail the firing position first.

A good position is shown on Plate 3. A right-handed man will place the butt into his right shoulder. This permits his right hand, which will be the more highly trained and responsive, to operate the safety catch and the triggers. The left hand lies along the barrels and plays the major part in aiming the gun. The right hand encircles and holds firmly the 'hand' or small of the stock. It should be no further forward than is necessary for it to reach the front trigger (which operates the right hand barrel) comfortably. This position has the double advantage that the finger is not cramped when it drops back onto the rear trigger, and the second finger is kept as clear as possible of the trigger guard. If it is too close the guard will strike it when the gun recoils, and can cause

▲20 Pigeons dropping into decoys as viewed from a straw bale hide. Notice how the stubble has been scythed down so the decoys show clearly. The Gun is firing at one of the higher pigeons so that his second shot will be at a lower, easier, bird.

▼21 A fraction of a second before this photograph was taken the pigeon was struck by the shot.

22   An unusually close view of a wood pigeon.

severe bruising. The thumb operates the safety catch, and must be slid off the top of the stock the instant this is done. This not only permits the right hand to take a firmer hold but prevents the top lever driving into the thumb on recoil.

The left hand is cupped around the underside of the barrels, and it is amusing to observe the vast variety of positions adopted. Do not be misled by the chequering on the fore-end into thinking that this is the correct hand hold. Ideally the left arm should be nearly straight, but if this position is adopted for firing at ground game the hand will have to be slid back for air shots. The best procedure is to point at an imaginary bird directly overhead, sliding the left hand forward until it is almost straight. This is the position in which the arm will be most extended, and if this hold is adopted permanently then the hand need never be moved. My enthusiasm for achieving a constant position may seem excessive at this time, but if you are ultimately to make successful snap shots the gun must always be held and mounted in the same fashion. Neither the thumb nor the fingers of the left hand will obtrude across the top of the barrels but they will rise a little on either side. Far from being a disadvantage these slight projections may even be sub-consciously used by some men as a preliminary aiming guide in the same way as the external hammers in old guns. The barrels should rest easily in the cup of the hand, but just before the shot is taken the grip of the thumb and the fingers should be tightened to help absorb the recoil. Some writers on marksmanship advise laying the left fore-finger in the groove between the barrels and using it to point at the target. My own experience is that this does nothing for my accuracy and leaves me with a sore finger.

The butt should be well up in the shoulder, which, as the right arm is curving forward to the triggers, will naturally form a convenient curve with the body into which to seat the butt. The head will be dropped sufficiently to rest the cheek on the comb of the stock and to bring the eye into position. This is not looking along the flat of the barrels so that all that is seen is the foresight, but a position slightly above. If the gun fits reasonably well, and the stock is kept well up in the shoulder, it will not be necessary to drop the head far. Taking a horizontal line through the shoulders the gun does not point away from this at 90 degrees. Such a position would be both uncomfortable and ugly. The ideal angle is a matter of personal preference but most shots prefer an angle of about 45 degrees.

It requires little thought to appreciate that in shooting moving targets the gun must be aimed and swung quickly and fluently, and to achieve this your feet must be correctly positioned and the body well balanced. Here again personal preference must play a part, but practically all the best shots keep the weight well forward. Personally I stand with my weight entirely on my left leg, with only the ball and toes of my right foot on the ground and acting simply as a means of steadying the body. This allows my body to pivot freely and easily with the movement spread from the hips and downwards – the gun is not moved horizontally from its relationship with the chest and shoulders. It is a common mistake to allow the weight to fall back onto the right foot when taking high shots. There is no need for this, even in shots past the vertical. The angles at which the feet point are not terribly important provided that they do not curtail the swing. I keep my left foot pointing a little anti-clockwise of right angles to the shoulders, and the right foot at right angles. Of course all these suggestions and rules pre-suppose ideal conditions in which the Gun has time to adopt the best posture. The wildfowler crouching in a muddy creek, or the rough shooter with a chance of a snap shot often has to fire from the most ridiculous positions. I once achieved a memorable right and left at wigeon whilst lying flat on my back.

An additional reason for keeping the weight forward is to help absorb the recoil which, at least with a 12 bore, is considerable. If you have never fired a shotgun before you will be wise to fire the first few into safe ground so that you may concentrate your mind upon taking a correct and firm hold. If you do not you may well suffer a bruised cheek, shoulder, or fingers, and develop a habit of flinching for months afterwards. The gun should be held firmly *to* the shoulder, but not pulled *into* it. There is no point in assisting the recoil, and your hold should be calculated to resist not assist it. Some writers recommend actually pushing against the recoil, but until you are very experienced all your concentration will be devoted to aiming.

Having discussed the firing position we will now consider how to get the gun to it. One of the distinguishing features between a good and a bad shot is the 'wildness' of the latter's barrels. They never seem to be still, wandering about as he walks or stands, and even if they are never dangerously pointed they move throughout the entire range of safe positions in a short time. And when the time comes to mount his gun the route his barrels follow in the process is never consistent. Conversely the barrels of the good shot are always neatly and tidily manipulated, inconspicuous until the target appears and then moving no more than is necessary.

The importance of good gun mounting is so great that it is well worthwhile devoting some time to perfecting a good technique. Read the following advice several times and then practise mounting your gun at a variety of static marks. Pigeon decoying gives excellent live practice, as the bird is in view for some time and the act of mounting can be carried out slowly and deliberately. Do not be content with your technique but constantly analyse and, if necessary, vary your performance. At the beginning it is much more necessary to shoot correctly than to hit the target – accuracy will improve, but bad habits once ingrained are there for ever.

For the novice the natural reaction on spotting the target is to put the butt to the shoulder, when in fact this is almost the last act of the sequence. The first movement is a dual one involving both extremities of the gun – the butt is moved into a position between the biceps of the right arm and the body, and the tips of the barrels are aligned between the eyes and the target. While this movement is taking place the brain is deciding on range, speed, direction and safety angles, and positioning the feet and body accordingly. For any given target there will be an ideal spot, be it in the ground or in the air, at which it should be shot. This may be determined by many factors – a gap in the trees, the safest position, the nearest point – but the good shot will know where he intends to kill the quarry, and at that point he will fire. A beginner can frequently be seen chasing the target with his barrels and firing at any point at which he thinks the aim is correct.

As the target approaches the killing point the left hand will quietly ease the gun forward until the butt can lift up into line with the shoulder. It is not yet, however, fully bedded into position. Meanwhile the barrels' tips have remained firmly attached to the target, and the moment of firing is near.

You may reasonably comment that it is premature to consider the business of firing the gun before it is fully mounted, but the majority of good shots believe that the gun should be fired at the instant the butt makes firm contact with the shoulder. Notice that I write 'majority' of good shots, and not 'all', for some prefer to mount the gun fully at an early stage. This technique may well be best for men of a slower more deliberate nature, and it is certainly easier for the beginner. You will probably find that this is the method you adopt at the beginning, but as you improve, and particularly when you take snap shots, you will find the time interval between bedding the butt and pulling the trigger decreasing. At this stage it is well worth while experimenting with the 'fire as you bed' technique.

While this digression has occurred the barrel tips have remained glued to the target, faithfully tracking its path and fractionally behind. If the target is a bird the eyes and brain are also assessing any curl in the flight path, or drift caused by a strong side wind. In either of these two eventualities (or even worse a combination of both) the aim will have to be 'laid off' a little to one side to compensate. As the target approaches the killing point the barrels speed up to reach and then overtake the target. At the same instant the butt slides home, the trigger is pulled and the shot is fired.

You will notice how much emphasis I have placed on swinging the gun, and it is equally important to keep the gun swinging for a short distance after the shot has been taken. The purpose of this is partly to assist in aiming and partly to avoid the shooting sin known as 'poking'. Poking, at its worst, consists of pointing a stationary gun at a spot you expect the target to reach and pulling the trigger a little before it gets there. In practice only the merest novice would do this, and the term usually describes the fault of halting the swing as the shot is fired, resulting in a miss behind. However, the main reason for swinging the gun is concerned with the subject of lead or, as it is sometimes known, forward allowance. Although the shot travels very quickly the target will have travelled several feet in the time it takes the shot to pass from the gun to the point of impact. Therefore the point of aim must be in front of the target if a miss behind is to be avoided. You will notice that in describing the act of firing in the previous paragraph I referred to the barrels overtaking the target. This gives the necessary forward allowance or lead to compensate for the time lag, but a little thought will show that the distance allowed must vary with the speed, distance and angle of travel of the target. The subject of lead is so important that the next chapter is devoted to it.

I have dealt with the whole action of mounting and firing the gun in slow and deliberate steps, and read in cold print it sounds fairly simple. In practice everything happens in a flash and you are unlikely to remember even lifting the gun, never mind the precise details of how you did so. This is why it is so important to have some preliminary practice. If you deliberately train yourself to follow the right procedure then you will do this instinctively. Certainly your brain will be far too busy identifying the target, estimating range, bothering about safety angles, and considering the forward allowance to think of correct mounting techniques. Unless this is done automatically you will quickly develop bad habits.

Rifle shots will wish to close one eye but this is not only unnecessary but bad. For the right shoulder shot the open left eye not only assists in estimating range, but registers the position of the target when it is necessarily blotted out by the barrels. As an example this occurs when the barrels are swung through an oncoming bird.

Some people criticize practice at clay pigeons on the grounds that they are unrealistic. Clays, the argument runs, start fast and slow down, whereas wild creatures do the reverse. This is true if you wait until the clay has travelled some distance, but taken reasonably early clay pigeons are a superb form of practice. Because you can control where and when the target will fly you can adjust your feet, vary your balance and practice mounting for a particular shot before you call for the clay. If you miss it you can repeat it time after time until you solve the problem. The best and fastest way to learn to shoot is unquestionably practice at clay pigeons accompanied by a professional coach. He will not only correct faults in your technique but tell you where each shot has missed and why. You will learn more in a morning with a professional than in a whole season of self-tuition.

From my earliest beginnings with a gun I kept a game book in which I recorded not only the bag but the number of cartridges I had fired. Apart from the pleasure of reviving old memories such a record provides an opportunity of checking the percentage of kills to cartridges and to observe the improvement in one's marksmanship that experience will bring. But do not be depressed if the increase is not dramatic for as you improve you will take difficult half-chances that previously you would have allowed to pass by. The desire to improve is natural and entirely laudable but beware of ruining your pleasure by letting misses depress you overmuch. I have shot with men whose entire day has been ruined because they were off form. The colour of the autumn leaves – the lunchtime laughter – the gloss on the coat of a dog in supreme condition – all these pleasures and many more have escaped them simply because they could not shoot straight.

Finally take heart in the thought that the next Gun is not really concerned about whether you will miss your next chance or not – he is far too bothered about his own performance.

In my view the best book available on this aspect of shooting is *Shotgun Marksmanship* by Stanbury and Carlisle, published by Herbert Jenkins.

Chapter 8

THE MYSTERY OF LEAD

This chapter owes its title to the fact that a surprising number of experienced shooting men cannot explain precisely what factors influence the amount of lead, or to use the better description, forward allowance, which is required. There is, in practice, no real call for them to have the theory at their fingertips, for there is no time to make any calculations when a wigeon comes hurtling down the tide edge, or a grouse flits over the hill. Just as a tennis player hits a moving ball without any mental arithmetic but with a sense of timing developed by long experience, so will the good shot vary the amount of lead instinctively.

Given ample opportunities and cartridges the beginner can also learn by trial and error, but he will learn much more quickly if he has a basic understanding of the problem. A simple example will illustrate this. In the time it takes the shot from a standard cartridge to travel 40 yards a bird flying at 40 m.p.h. will have travelled 8 feet. As the effective spread of a cartridge is only 30 inches if the gun is pointed straight at the bird the charge will miss by almost 7 feet. Even as close as 30 yards the allowance at this speed has to be over 5 feet. Nor is this the end of the problem for these allowances only compensate for the time taken for the shot to travel from the gun to the target – they take no account of the human delay which occurs from the time the brain reads the message of the eye and instructs the trigger finger to fire. It is at this stage that many men become muddled and settle for letting instinct take control. You, good reader, will I trust persevere for the matter is less complicated than first appears.

The total delay, from the instant the eye observes that the gun is in the correct position in relation to the target to the moment that the shot strikes, can be divided into two quite separate intervals – the human and the mechanical. The human ranges from the action of the eye to the instant that the hammer, released when the finger pulls the trigger, ignites the cartridge cap. The mechanical from the ignition of the cap to the arrival of the shot at the target. The mechanical delay has the advantage that the sequences up to the point where the shot leaves the barrel take an identical, if very brief, period of time for each shot. The remainder of the mechanical delay, the flight of the shot, varies in proportion to the distance it has to cover, but because the distance is readily observed it is a simple matter to allow a longer lead for longer ranges. The human delay, however, is not constant, principally because the central performer is a human. He may be fresh or tired, fit or ill, alert or groggy from the lunchtime food or drink. He may have cold fingers, a thorn in his boot, or be cross with his wife. To formulate the correct allowance for the human element of delay is impossible. It is indeed fortunate that it is also unnecessary.

In the previous chapter I laid high stress on the need to maintain the swing, and a moment's thought should show that if this is done the human delay is automatically eliminated. Imagine, if you will, the target flying across the sky with the barrels travelling ahead of it and leading it by the distance necessary to eliminate the mechanical delay only. Imagine that the eye tells the brain the lead is correct, the brain passes the message to the finger, and the finger pulls the trigger. A fraction of time will have passed but whether it is 3/1000 second or 30/1000 second is of no consequence provided that the swing has been maintained. At the instant that the mechanical sequence begins the lead will still be the correct amount necessary to eliminate it.

From this we learn the vital rule that provided the swing is maintained the element of human delay can be ignored. It is only when 'poking' begins that the human delay plays a part. This also explains why, again in the previous chapter, I wrote that it is easier for the novice to put the butt to the shoulder and swing with the target. Bedding the butt and firing in the same moment brings a measure of the human delay into the lead factor.

If you find your shooting deteriorates the answer will very frequently be found in a failure to maintain the swing. You may feel confident you are swinging but it is easy to tense and slow the swing as you fire. This is why I wrote previously of the need to continue the swing for a little after the shot has been made. You will now understand my anxiety at the beginning of this chapter for you to understand the factors involved in lead. It is only by so doing that one can analyse one's mistakes, and intelligently consider the remedies.

Proper swinging, therefore, reduces the need for lead simply to the compensation for the time that the shot takes on its journey from the instant it leaves the barrels (and therefore your control) to its arrival. How do we calculate this compensation? Returning to the bird flying at 40 m.p.h. and crossing at right-angles, the necessary lead can vary from a little over 4 feet at 25 yards to 11 feet at 50 yards. Unfortunately targets do not all travel at 40 m.p.h. or cross at right-angles, and we certainly cannot be sure of their range. This is one of the elements of shooting in which instinct, trained by experience, takes control over reason. The most my conscious brain ever contributes to success is to transmit rough messages on the lines of 'this is a really fast one – give it plenty of lead', or 'it's hanging in the wind – only a little lead'. Although the good shot will never actually estimate his lead in feet the novice, faced with a straightforward crossing shot, may find it helpful to try. It is, after all, pointless to call on instinctive experience if you have none. The immediate problem, however, is estimating what 9 feet, for example, looks like at 40 yards. The answer is to relate it to the quarry. For instance, give a cock pheasant at 40 yards four times its own length (I know this is nearer 12 feet than 9 but you want to hit him in the head not the tail!).

The most common error with inexperienced shots is to miss behind, and if you are failing to connect try increasing the lead – even to the point where it appears excessive. A frequent, and successful, gambit of the professional coach is to ask the unsuccessful shot to try to miss in front. You will soon gain enough experience to judge the lead necessary for straightforward crossing shots, and the next step is to learn to assess rapidly the lead necessary for each of the tremendous variety of angles at which targets can present themselves. I repeat that it is impossible to make assessments in terms of feet, but a rapid decision of the flight path and whether a large or small lead is needed is a great start for instinct.

We have already considered the bird presenting a simple crossing shot, but in many cases it will be not only crossing but rising or falling.

73

In this event the lead will be not only in front but also a little above or below. It is worth while sitting down at a table, with some small object to represent the target, and working out where the shot will have to be placed in various situations. With a bird flying directly away the lead is given by firing underneath it; while for ground game running directly away the aim will be over the top. Oncoming birds will be blotted out by the barrels, while the shot will be directed at the feet of oncoming ground game. A little consideration of these and other situations will teach you a great deal about lead. Remember that the speed that concerns us is not the speed of the target through the air but the speed relative to the barrels of the gun. A grouse approaching head on at 60 m.p.h. needs no lead at all – the shot is fired directly at it. Again a pheasant flying away from you at an angle of 45 degrees needs only half the lead of a pheasant at the same distance crossing at right angles at the same speed.

When you consider that a pheasant can be crossing at an angle of 30 degrees whilst also gliding and falling and curling in a side wind, or a wigeon can be climbing away from you with little forward speed but a gale force wind from one side, you will see how impossible accurate calculation is. Lead, if you think deeply about it, is informed instinct.

Chapter 9

ON FINDING SHOOTING

For many shooting beginners the problem of where to shoot looms far larger than such technical considerations as the size of gun to buy, or the lead needed for a bird crossing at 40 m.p.h. Most novices would be delighted to have the chance to shoot a bird crossing at any speed with any gun. Quite obviously as the population grows and the countryside shrinks under concrete, tarmac and bricks the pressure for shooting rights increases. Old books on shooting never mentioned the problem of finding ground; the problem just did not exist. Now it is so considerable that except for the fortunate few with rural contacts it is the major obstacle for the beginner.

The answers depend very largely upon whether or not you can afford to pay for your sport. Let us consider first the opportunities awaiting the more financially fortunate.

The simple, but most expensive, approach is to read the advertisement columns of the field sports magazines. Some of the ground offered is good value for money, and some rubbish, but the mere fact that the owners have gone to the expense and trouble of advertising it suggests that they intend to obtain its full worth, and possibly more. The next step down is the advertisement columns of the rural county press, and finally comes personal contact. The personal contact procedure is the same as that used by the beginners with no available money so the details can wait while we consider how to assess the ground offered.

In fact the majority of advertisements will offer a gun in a syndicate rather than ground, mainly because the demand for ground is so great that it is rarely necessary to advertise it. It would be very wrong for a complete novice to take a syndicate Gun, for not only would he be unfamiliar with the procedures but he would stand an excellent chance of killing someone. The ideal number of companions for the novice shot is one. This is all he needs to gain help and advice, and any more increases the danger. However a sensible man will quite quickly become a safe shot, so at the end of this chapter I give advice on joining a syndicate. Returning to renting ground rather than a syndicate Gun, I would advise against paying a substantial rent for your first shoot even if the ground is well worth it. There is a lot to be learned and a great many mistakes to be made yet, and it is pointless to have ground well stocked with game if your lack of knowledge and experience prevents you getting to within range of more than a small fraction, most of which you promptly miss. Nor will you learn the most if you rent ground of one character only. The ideal is a small mixed rough shoot offering a variety of both quarry and habitat. Arable fields with alternating crops to bring the pheasants to the stubble and the pigeons to the clover leys; thick hedges with ample nesting cover for game, and big oak trees to shed their acorns and hold the pheasants when the stubbles are ploughed in; an old wood with a stand of larches where the pigeons can be flighted, and a woodcock occasionally flushed from the bracken at the edge. And finally to this rough shooter's heaven we must add a few water meadows with a brook upon which the odd mallard or teal may be found, with a spring that stays unfrozen in hard weather to attract the snipe for miles around. This is the kind of ground made for rough shooters, not rolling acres of cultivated prairie. You will be more than lucky if you find ground with one half the facilities I have listed, but it will do for a start. There is so much more to shooting than firing a gun, and the first season or so is well spent simply pottering quietly around watching, listening, observing and getting off the occasional shot.

You are unlikely to be given figures of previous seasons' bags with a rough shoot. Telephoning the previous tenant is one fairly sound approach, but in these days there is often no time; the shoot is taken overnight. I recall walking round a Sheppey freshwater marsh in high summer with cattle and sheep grazing peacefully in all directions while the owner assured me that in winter it was covered with water and duck. An immediate decision was required. I liked his eyes, said yes, and enjoyed seven years of great sport. However, it could have gone the other way and snap decisions are better avoided where possible. Where you are inexperienced in the haunts of game there is a good case to be made for assessing the man rather than the ground. A farmer who will be meeting you regularly through the year is unlikely to deceive you.

It is very difficult to advise on rents, partly because inflation makes nonsense of any facts given in books that will remain in print for some time. At the moment good shooting ground will readily fetch a pound an acre, and it will inevitably creep up. This is why so little comes on the market, for those who enjoy a small shoot at a sensible rent stick to it. Cost was the spur behind the rapid growth of the syndicate, and it is also the reason why nowadays even rough shoots are usually taken by a small group of friends. Three or four men, each throwing in say £50, can hope to find a modest shoot. A man on his own with £50 will be lucky to find more than a few fields. But do not despair – it can be done. Some very good rough shooting is still rented for small sums.

Judged by the foregoing, the second group, those unable to pay a rent, have no hope. In practice tenacity and a willing smile will get results. The art is to offer to shoot those creatures that other people often want shot. This usually means hares and pigeons, but as a hare shoot is no place for a beginner then the pigeons are the answer. And no mean answer; there is as much fun to be had in shooting pigeons as any other form of shooting. There are two occasions when pigeon shooting can often be had for the asking; when they are ravaging a crop, and when an entire area is being covered for pigeon roost flighting. In the first case the farmer is losing money fast, and in the second there is nearly always a shortage of Guns to cover all the woods. Naturally it is essential to know of these situations but this is where the tenacity comes in. A reconnaissance in October to see which farm has sprouts which will turn blue with pigeons when snow covers their other feeding is a simple act of initiative which may pay well.

Remember that you have to help a farmer only once and do it well, and you may have pigeon shooting for life. Of course consent will be more readily given if it is sought in the right way. A car screeching up to the farm door from which several young men emerge dressed like budding cowboys and clutching guns is obviously wrong. Ideally one should get to know the local farmers in some way and gain a reputation for reliability. One often successful approach is to work as a beater in local shoots, for this way you come to know the keepers who can often introduce you to a farmer who will permit pigeon shooting. Or offer them a hand on the rearing fields next summer, and when the shoots are over help hang up the birds instead of getting paid and disappearing. All this may sound a lot of trouble, but all conjuring tricks involve trouble and there is no greater conjuring trick than producing rough shooting with no money.

Involve yourself with country people in country activities. Help them where you can, sincerely, and not for what you can immediately gain; be patient and in time you will be surprised how many doors will open. I came to Surrey twenty years ago knowing no-one and with no money. On my first free day I set out southwards and simply called at every farm I passed seeking permission to shoot pigeons. The fifth agreed and for two years I enjoyed fair sport. Then I suggested I should rear a few pheasants, the idea was well received, and over the years I have shot several hundred birds there. Nor is this an isolated story. In the course of a year I shoot widely over Norfolk, Suffolk, Lincolnshire, Cambridgeshire, Kent, Surrey, Sussex, Hampshire and the Hebrides. In some cases I pay, but in many I enjoy the hospitality of good friends – all found by being involved in the countryside. The old saying that the more you put into life the more you get out of it applies equally well to shooting.

Once you feel you have enough experience to shoot safely, and if you can afford it, there is a great deal of sport and pleasure to be had from joining a syndicate. It is a simple business to make contact through advertisements, but when you meet the captain never try to deceive him over your limited experience. Before long you will give yourself away and he will never forgive you. Far better, when the question of experience is raised by the captain (and if it is not you should have doubts about joining) to say quite bluntly, 'I've been shooting for only so long. My shooting has been done with Bill Brown who has been shooting all his life, and he has been very strict with me. I'm very conscious of the need for safety, and would always treat it as paramount. If I join I would be only too pleased if you would correct me if

I transgress in any way.' Any sane captain should be more willing to have you in the team than some elderly man who has shot recklessly for forty years, thinks he knows it all, and is quite beyond correction.

However, if you are too readily accepted in spite of your rawness, then take heed. It might be a bad syndicate in which the captain cannot afford to be over selective. In general terms syndicates may be judged like men – as they have performed in the past so are they likely to perform in the future. As you are being asked to part with money you are perfectly entitled to ask for the records of previous years. No further time should be wasted with the man who says he has mislaid the game book and cannot remember the exact figures. There is an increasing tendency for unscrupulous farmers and other landowners close to big towns to form syndicates which promise a great deal, collect a sizeable subscription from each Gun and then, when the bag is very low, say that it must be the weather, the foxes and a dozen other rural disasters. Fortunately there is a simple precaution against this. If the syndicate is a good one the Guns remain members; if not, they leave. The resignation of a Gun or occasionally two a season is permissible. If the turnover rate is high have nothing to do with the place. Another trap, less easily detected, is the good syndicate about to suffer a change. Is a really good keeper leaving, or a motorway coming through the main covert next Spring? Obviously nothing beats personal recommendation, but where there is no contact and you have reservations it is worth asking the captain if he minds you telephoning one or two of the other Guns. He may object but he can hardly say so. Try to discover whether all the expenses are split equally between the Guns, or whether the captain rents the ground, takes all the financial responsibility and then tries to let Guns at such a figure that he enjoys free shooting. There is no real objection to this – if a man shoulders the entire responsibility he is entitled to benefit, but it is a system that does not always make for the happiest relationships between the Guns.

Chapter 10

FIELDCRAFT AND BEHAVIOUR

If you are both to enjoy your shooting to the full and at the same time be accepted by the other people of the countryside, you must have a sound knowledge of these two aspects of shooting. It is, of course, possible to blunder forth quite ignorant of either, but the penalty for lacking fieldcraft is a reduced bag and/or discomfort, and for behaving badly, unpopularity and possibly, dreadful thought, a shooting invitation not renewed.

I spent some time trying to think of a brief definition for fieldcraft, but this is not easy for the subject covers such a vast range. Such an obvious act as detecting the alarm call of a blackbird deep in the wood and freezing by a tree in case a fox trots through comes under this heading. But equally does not the man who carefully mounts the Guns' trailer so that he sits with his back to the wind and keeps his hands warm, the better to handle his gun, also practice fieldcraft? True countrymen, who do not necessarily live in the country, are easily picked out. They have an alertness of eye, a quietness of voice, and an ability to look right in their surroundings. If you are new to the country scene study them carefully, for there is much to be learnt from them. I suppose fieldcraft might be described as the art of achieving one's purpose outdoors, with the minimum of discomfort, and in the process observing all but causing no unnecessary damage or noise.

As dressing correctly has to be done before leaving home this is a convenient starting point. It is a rare occasion in Britain that one can set out for a full day confident that there will be no rain, and therefore the basis of all outdoor outfits should be a reliable waterproof jacket. Wet legs are acceptable, but once the trunk is soaked the day is miserable. As the difference in weight between a showerproof jacket and one that is fully waterproof is negligible common sense dictates the latter. There are various fully waterproof materials available, of which

▲23 Setting out the decoys in front of a bale hide.

▼24 This gunner found a sticky spot in the creek bottom and was lucky to escape with a wetting.

25   Dawn on the Wash. A mallard to hand and the sun breaking through a sea mist.

the plastics cause sweating and the nylons are prone to tear on wire or thorns. It is possible to spend anything from £5 to £40 on a shooting jacket, but personally I would never pay more than was necessary to obtain a sound item. There is little place in the country for sartorial splendour. Nor would I buy a jacket that lacked a removable hood, for in severe weather this is a great asset. If you spend much time outdoors it is useful to have two jackets; a light one for wet summer or mild winter days, and a heavy one for the wicked weather. The same reasoning applies to over-trousers. On the days when the rain is obviously continuous a thick substantial pair is essential, but for showery weather a light nylon pair which can be carried in the pocket is ideal. A light pair may be fully waterproof when new but they will not stand up to the brambles and wire encountered in prolonged use.

There is a delightful informality in dress among the shooting fraternity, the main rule being that of picking clothes that are sensible for the job on hand. Even in a formal syndicate there is an informal freedom that will see one Gun in smart tweeds and heavy shoes and the next in a wildfowling smock and Wellingtons. This is not an encouragement for scruffiness in the shooting field, but an expression of my personal belief that shooting men as a whole are not over concerned with the niceties of dress. Obviously one will dress to suit the day, and in the course of a season I vary from plus twos and long stockings, to walking over the remoter hills of the Hebrides in shorts with my toes poking out through a pair of old tennis shoes.

Headgear provides scope for individuality. The main point to remember is that its least important function is decoration. Essentially it should provide warmth, keep the sun from the eyes, and water from the neck. The cap does most of these things and is less likely to be blown off than a hat, but it does little to stop rain pouring down the sides and back of the neck. It is difficult to imagine a more practical headpiece than the Scottish 'fore and aft', and it was evolved in a country where men know about these things. Footwear is almost a subject in its own right. Briefly you will be happier in leather boots, but dryer in Wellingtons. I wear boots whenever practical, but on the really wet days there is no alternative to rubbers if you are to maintain dry feet. On the assumption that wet days are frequently also cold days it is good sense to buy Wellingtons of a size that will permit two pairs of socks.

The outfit I have discussed so far has been concerned with keeping you dry, but wetness is only part of the problem of being outdoors in hard weather – we must consider the cold. The extent to which you must dress to resist cold is determined largely by the activity you will pursue. The man who will be active, for example, the rough shooter, can dress relatively lightly, but the static shooter who will be decoying pigeons or waiting for driven pheasants will need very much more clothing if he is to remain warm. The principle is to imitate the ducks who have a layer of hard, waterproof feathers on the outside and a thick layer of fluffy air-filled down underneath. There are many types of clothing which are suitable to form the human equivalent of the down, and obviously wool is an excellent material. Most countrymen swear by some particular medium which may vary from a moleskin waistcoat to sheets of newspaper, but I am content to pile on a good thickness of woollen vests, shirts and pullovers. Do not neglect the legs. It is nonsense to cover the top half with several layers of clothing and expect the legs to remain warm with a single pair of trousers. Ignore the comments of the females in your life and buy a pair of long woollen underpants. Two pairs of socks are essential in hard weather.

Many men fail to appreciate the considerable heat loss that occurs from the neck and wrists, with the clothes acting as a pump every time the arms are raised and lowered. In severe conditions a silk scarf round the neck and mittens on the hands reduce the loss, and are also very warming to the exposed skin. Mittens have the great advantage for the shooter that the fingers and palms are left uncovered and the feel of the gun is preserved. If you must wear gloves cut a slit in the trigger finger of them.

It hardly needs to be said that the colour of all the items you wear should be quiet and tone in with the colours of the countryside. An advantage of a hat or cap with a brim is that it helps to conceal the big white blob of the face.

Colour, movement and noise are the three factors most likely to alarm the wild creatures, and of these noise is the greatest sin. The sounds of a closing gate, or the scrape of a boot on a stone are bad, but worst of all is the human voice which will alert all wildlife within hearing. Some will slink quickly away down hedge or ditch, some will disappear into their holes, beneath the water or wherever they go in a crisis, and the rest will hide. He who speaks over-frequently will move in barren countryside. Good rough shooters will hardly ever communicate by voice but with signs or the occasional whistle. Common sense dictates the need to select clothing of colours which will merge with the surroundings, but where the maximum camouflage is needed the hands and face should be covered. For the latter, cheap face masks can be purchased which do the job well. Alternatively the less fastidious can use the old wildfowler's trick of rubbing on a handful of mud. Movement alarms wild creatures more than colour, and you should take advantage of every available natural feature. This is not to suggest you crawl up every convenient ditch for no obvious purpose. I am simply proposing that you advertise your presence as little as possible, and you may reap a bonus in the shape of a flock of pigeons suddenly looming over the hedge, or a cock pheasant which freezes in the stubble when you appear at 40 yards instead of legging it for the wood, as it would have done had you been sighted at half a mile. It is just a question of keeping tight to a hedge instead of walking across the centre of a field, or sticking to the valley instead of the crest of the hill. Whenever the quarry is in sight and heading for you absolute stillness is vital. For instance, if you spot a pigeon or a party of duck approaching do not drop into cover – freeze. This way there is a good chance they will pass over, but the movement of taking cover will almost invariably alarm them.

Experienced countrymen are always observant, registering a thousand details which would go unnoticed by the townsman. To them our apparently barren countryside has many stories to tell; some, like the droppings of a fox, calling for action; and others, for instance, the slot of a roe deer, arousing only interest. Only days before he died I was fishing the Itchen with Oliver Kite, the fisherman and naturalist whose television programmes attracted a large following. I found him gazing thoughtfully across the river at a lush water meadow, 'John, my boy,' he said, 'there are six different shades of green in that meadow.' This quality of observation is doubly useful for the shooting man, for it not only permits greater enjoyment of the country, but helps to fill the bag. The rural Sherlock Holmes spots the signs of mallard in the stubble, and is waiting at dusk, or notes the build up of a pigeon flight-line beneath the shelter of a beech belt as the wind strengthens. He also watches his fellow men and learns where the duck have been flighting from the pile of empty cases not quite fully thrust beneath the mud by an impatient wader, or spots and follows the little band of knowledge-able locals nipping quietly off to the flank at the hare shoot. A sharp eye and a quick brain contribute towards a successful shooter.

It hardly needs saying that the first rule of correct behaviour is the strict observance of all the safety rules laid down in Chapter 6. But these are just the foundations of a good reputation, and there is much more to observe. The late Hugh Monahan, a past President of WAGBI, once said, 'A wildfowler should shoot like a gentleman.' So indeed should every shooting man, and every rule of behaviour is based on this, plus some common sense.

The need to display good shooting manners is obviously more pressing for the man who is one of a party than the lone wolf, and the first rule for the gregarious shot is to be on time. To keep others waiting for no good reason is inexcusable. There is another definition of 'waiting', in the context of shooting, which involves correct be-haviour, and this is whether or not you wait for a neighbouring Gun to take first shot at a target within range of you both. In some rough shoots there may be an understanding that no-one waits for another Gun, but in most shoots, and certainly in formal driven shoots, it is wrong to poach a shot which is obviously closer to another Gun. 'Browning' is also ungentlemanly shooting and is the crime of firing not at a single bird but into the centre or 'brown' of a group of several. Typical targets for this misdemeanour are a covey of grouse or a flight of teal. Incidentally the main offence here is that such shots almost in-variably lead to wounded birds. It is wrong to fire near stock or the general public even if the angle is such that no danger exists. Both will be frightened. Gentlemen do not take long shots in the hope that a chance stray pellet will break a wing bone or damage a vital organ. If the target is not close enough to kill cleanly it should be left alone for otherwise it is far more likely to be 'pricked' than bagged. At all formal shoots, and even the moderately organized informal ones, once you are placed in a spot stay there until recalled. It may look wrong to you but the organizer knows his ground, and straying is dangerous. When you make a kill mark the fall carefully, particularly if it is in some featureless country such as a field of sugar beet. It is no use having a vague idea; you must be able to say 'five yards to the right of that clump of thistles', or something equally definite. Few things are more irritating to the dog owner than the Gun who screams for a dog and then vaguely flaps his hand at a vast expanse of cover.

When shooting casually it is sensible to make sure the farmer or keeper knows of your presence. If not they may waste time when they hear a gun fired or see people in the distance. On new ground discover the local policy on foxes. There is no area where the locals are in-different – they either want them all shot or will ostracize you for life if you so much as aim at one. At formal shoots some owners and keepers object to a gun being fired before the signal to start the drive is given. At others once the Guns are at their pegs there is no objection to a welcome being given to any passing pigeon or magpie. If you shoot as a guest always check whether or not hen pheasants are being shot once Christmas is past. Never take a dog out with other Guns if you cannot control it, or to a driven shoot a dog which whines at the peg. It will distract not only you but your neighbours. If you have wounded the quarry you should persevere until you find it, and only the most pressing reasons permit you to give up the search. Even then you should either return yourself as soon as possible, or arrange for someone else to do so. Once retrieved wounded game must be killed instantly and firmly. With birds the most humane and quickest method is to break the neck with a rapid twist culminating, when resistance is felt, with a quick pull. Snipe can be killed very quickly by pressing in the skull with the thumbnail. Rabbits and hares should be killed by sus-pending them by the back legs and striking them firmly behind the ears with the flat of the hand. Do not attempt to kill pheasants by holding their head only and whirling the body round. It is ugly to watch, demeans the quarry and does not always work.

Chapter 11

ROUGH SHOOTING

Rough shooting means hunting over mixed ground for any legitimate quarry which can be found. It can involve walking the hills in Scotland for grouse, hares and snipe, or a small farm in Norfolk for pheasants, rabbits and pigeons. It can be practised by what I regard as the ideal combination, two friends with two dogs; by a lone shooter; or by a fairly sizeable party. Rough shooting shares with wildfowling the distinction of being a pure form of shooting in which the participants have no artificial assistance from beaters, but pit their wits and skills against the speed, eyesight and hearing of the quarry. As an activity it calls for a good knowledge of the countryside, fieldcraft, energy and, very often, patience and tenacity. Some of the most enthusiastic shooting men I know, who can readily afford a gun in a good driven shoot, still prefer the satisfaction of a small bag on a rough shoot.

In spite of the problems of finding a rough shoot many beginners start their shooting careers in this way. It is certainly the best, for a man will learn more knocking about a rough shoot for a season than in several years of shooting driven game. It is possible to break most of the rules of dress, noise and movement on a driven shoot and still have some sport, but not when rough shooting. The essential difference between driven and rough shooting is that in the former the quarry is brought to the Gun whereas in the latter he has to go out and find it. Rough shooting without a dog is possible, but impractical. It is also much less fun. Chapter 18 covers the subject of dogs.

No matter how quietly you may proceed some of the quarries will flee before you, and often so far in advance that you will never realize they have been there. I once shot a fresh water marsh in north Kent in severe weather, and a heavy snow blizzard forced me to hole up for several hours in a drain culvert. When it cleared I spotted my two companions, who had promised to join me later in the day, walking down to the marsh from the high ground. By this time none of the wild life on the marsh was aware of my presence, and when my friends were still over a mile away the various creatures started to move off. Quietly, purposefully and without panic they went. The hares loped along, stopping occasionally to sit erect and look back. Several coveys of partridges swept gracefully across the snow to settle well over the main creek, and a pair of cock pheasants trotted briskly along where the exposed slopes held the least snow. But for the tracks in the snow my friends could have been excused for thinking the marsh had been empty all day.

This situation can be avoided by shooting with a companion and planning one's moves carefully. The tactics are to carry out a pincer movement, so that those quarries which flee before you are within range, will move towards your companion and you, in turn, will benefit from the disturbance he creates. There is enormous satisfaction in carefully planning a move, like a General a battle plan, putting it into execution, and seeing it work. And even if it fails and a handful of pheasants burst prematurely from a flank, or a spring of teal lifts before the guns are within range, you will have learnt just a little more about one of the most absorbing and difficult forms of shooting.

I have already covered many aspects of fieldcraft, dress, gun safety, and marksmanship, all of which play a part in rough shooting, and the remainder of this chapter will be more usefully devoted to detailing the most common quarries, their characteristics, and the techniques of shooting each.

PIGEONS

The pigeon is such a universal and sporting target that many men concentrate on it to the almost complete exclusion of other species. The sport obtainable from it, and the skills necessary to come to terms with it, are such that I have devoted the whole of Chapter 13 to it.

PHEASANTS

There is no firm evidence to support the theory that the Romans first brought the pheasant from its home in Asia to Britain, but whoever introduced it rendered a great service to the shooting man. Given reasonable cover and natural food the pheasant not only survives but thrives, and the increase in rearing has assisted a population growth which means there are probably more pheasants in Britain today than ever before. The preference of a pheasant is to run rather than fly, and when pushing out thick cover it is essential to cover the last few feet very thoroughly. Quite often you will find that most of the birds have run forward and squatted. Cock pheasants show greater initiative and cunning than hens, and by January are most difficult to bag. If you have followed the same pattern of shooting throughout the season it sometimes pays to reverse, when the cocks, who by now have learnt the form, may come racing into trouble. Men who only shoot driven pheasants are sometimes guilty of deriding walked up pheasants as offering easy shots. A wet pheasant lumbering up from almost underfoot in sugar beet can be easy, but so can a low, early season hen flying slowly across in a driven shoot. In general a fair assessment is that in rough shooting the chances can vary from very easy to extremely difficult, whereas in driven shooting the majority of opportunities are moderately difficult. Remember that in rough shooting the bird has almost always just been flushed and is usually rising. As a result these chances are often missed below. For those men who make the mistake of shooting at the middle of the target rather than the head, the long tail of the cock pheasant causes many misses. The middle is a little aft of the stomach, and only a slight error will result in a few large feathers drifting earthwards and a bird disappearing at maximum speed.

RABBITS

Prominent among the golden days of my youth in Norfolk are memories of chasing rabbits across the long stubble of the harvest fields, as the binders clanked their way down the ever decreasing central wall of waving corn. Later, in the hills of Derbyshire, I spent many cruel winter days ferreting on the moors, often in falling snow. For me, as for many shooting men, the rabbit was the backbone of our sport. Like the pheasant it was introduced to this country, apparently about the end of the twelfth century, when it was kept in warrens for meat. It took some 300 years to break out and become really abundant, after which it became a considerable nuisance to farmers in many areas. Neither gun, net, nor trap could really subdue their numbers for long, but in the early 1950s the disease of myxomatosis devastated the species, producing some pathetic sights as blind and dying rabbits littered the countryside. The numbers probably fell to their lowest in 1954 and have since slowly recovered, but to nowhere near their pre-myxomatosis peak.

There are now few areas where the numbers warrant concentrating a day's shooting entirely on the rabbit, but the sudden explosion of a rabbit from cover is invariably great sport. In woodland particularly they will twist and jump, and make difficult shooting with the shooter, understandably, tending to miss behind. Ferreting is an interesting and enjoyable exercise but it is quite an art and you will be wise to spend a few days with an experienced hand rather than buying a ferret and plunging forth. The net result of such rashness will probably be to finish up with the ferrets teeth set firm in a finger. Where there is a good stock of rabbits it is worth 'stinking them out', to use the vernacular. The technique is to go round the day before you shoot with a good supply of balls of paper soaked overnight in paraffin. These are pushed down every hole but one in each warren. If all goes well the following day the rabbits will be found lying out, and can be walked up. Once dead a rabbit should be held up by the head, and the thumb of the free hand run firmly down the stomach. This expels any urine which would otherwise leak into the game bag. To assist in carrying or hanging a rabbit it should be 'legged' or 'hocked'. A knife slit is made in the left rear leg between the bone and the main tendon above what in a human would be the ankle joint, and the right leg threaded through.

HARES

The hare is a native of Britain and, depending for its safety on speed, is a creature of the open spaces. It rests in a 'form', which is usually a depression in thick grass or other vegetation, although on plough it will kick out a small hole into which the powerful rear legs and haunches lie. In the Scottish Highlands, Ireland and a few other limited areas the brown hare is replaced by the blue or mountain hare. This is smaller, with blue-grey fur which turns white in winter.

Although large hare shoots, which are usually held in February, frequently have bags running into hundreds the rough shooter will normally walk up only the occasional hare and this more often by chance than design. The target presented is most frequently going away, and it is vital to aim well over the top. Failure to do this can mean a hare with shattered rear legs, and there is no more heart rending sound in the shooting field than the cry of a wounded hare. Hares are large and powerful creatures and it is very wrong to take long shots at them. As I wrote in an earlier chapter one of the justifications of shooting is that, properly carried out, the quarry feels little or no pain. If you wound a hare which still has the capacity to move do not attempt to chase it. Use the second barrel and kill it at once. Hares should be 'watered' and legged in the same way as rabbits. Beware of shooting one, or more, if you have a long way to walk. I once shot seven at an early stage in a Cambridgeshire hare drive, and then had to carry them over half a mile across sticky plough. By the end I understood why the old farm hands on either side of me had seemed so slow to spot chances at the start.

DUCK

Are dealt with in detail in Chapter 15. Suffice to say that their existence is a great asset to any rough shoot.

PARTRIDGES

The little grey or English partridge is, at least in my view, one of the most attractive of birds. For reasons which the scientists are only just beginning to unravel, but which are basically connected with modern changes in farming practices, their numbers have dropped to a dangerous level in recent years. It is not an easy bird for the rough shooter to bag for it is usually up and away long before it is in range. However in roots, stubble, or thick cover it can be done. If you have the chance to shoot partridges I would urge you to consider whether the stocks in your area permit this. Our countryside would be much the poorer if the partridge went, and if you have any doubts stay your hand. The English partridge and the teal rank among the tastiest of all the shooting mens' quarries.

The red-legged partridge, sometimes called the 'Frenchman' is gaining in numbers. It is a little larger and more boldly marked with black and chestnut stripes on its flanks. It also differs in being less inclined to fly than the Grey, and on wet days not infrequently finishes up in the ridiculous position of clogging its feet so heavily with mud that it cannot fly, and can be picked up, cleaned and released.

WOODCOCK

Although considerable numbers of woodcock nest in this country they are reinforced each winter by the migrant birds which cross the North Sea. The long bill enables it to probe for earthworms and beetles and it must perforce find soft marshy ground to feed. The woodcock has a reputation for being a difficult bird to shoot, and for many years an internationally famous drink firm has given awards to those sportsmen who have accomplished a right and left each season. In fact when shot in the open it is no more difficult than any other bird. The problem lies in its love of woodlands in which it is obliged to fly irregularly in order to avoid the obstacles.

I propose making this one of the few books on general shooting which does not include the story of the long-lived keeper and his reaction to the shout of 'woodcock'.

There is no particular technique to be practised in shooting woodcock other than to exercise great care, for their habit of zigzagging through thick cover, often at face height, has led to many accidents. Ireland enjoys a large woodcock migration during the winter, and a combined wildfowling/woodcock shooting holiday there can be enormous fun.

COMMON SNIPE

The snipe is in many aspects a smaller version of the woodcock, sharing much the same varieties of food for which it probes in soft ground with a bill which makes up a quarter of its total length. Its fast and zigzagging flight offers a most difficult shot for the beginner, and I recall my eldest son being reduced to near tears when he first tried his hand at them. Unlike the woodcock the snipe avoids woodland, and is a bird of the marshes and water meadows. As with woodcock our resident population is swollen by Continental migrants in the autumn and winter. The general rule with all our visitors from the Continent is that the severer the weather over the Channel the greater the migration. Snipe are fairly kind to the shooter and allow a reasonably close approach before dashing off with a harsh cry which I find variously described in the bird books as 'scaup', 'scape' and 'creech'. Snipe are very sensitive to noise, and blundering heavily through the reeds or talking will send them off prematurely. Many words of advice have been written on how to shoot snipe, varying from those who advocate snap shooting to knock them down before they start to zigzag, to those who suggest waiting until the zigzagging stops. I have never followed either extreme. As the snipe commences evasive flight almost immediately it rises snap shooting is not only very difficult but can be dangerous – especially for the beginner who has to think about safety angles far longer than the experienced gun. Waiting for the flight to straighten means that the bird is often at extreme range before the shot can be taken. Although it may catch you out with a very rapid change I find the best technique is to mount the gun with a normal rhythm and fire immediately after it has made a change of direction. Snipe are one of the few quarries where I would advocate a departure from No. 6 shot, for they are so fragile that penetration is no problem, and the need is for the densest possible pattern. No. 8 is excellent, but should be used only if you are confident that the targets will be exclusively snipe. It is too light for the pheasants and duck which are frequently found in the snipe habitat. Waiting in the dusk for duck to flight you may be puzzled by a resonant, quavering, humming noise. This is a male snipe 'drumming' and is caused by the vibrating of two outer tail feathers of the snipe as it dives. In the North it has earned the bird the country name of 'heather bleater'. Finally a plea for sporting behaviour with the snipe. In spite of being fired at it will often settle again, sometimes after flying in a large circle, within a hundred yards or so. My view, and I hope you will share it, is that if you have had a chance at the bird and missed then you should leave it in peace.

GROUSE

Contrary to popular belief many grouse are shot by walking up, and wonderful sport it is too. Chapter 16 on moorland shooting, covers the subject in detail.

PREDATORS

Not so many years ago the policy of gamekeepers was to kill every bird and beast capable of killing game birds whether adult or in the egg. On those estates sufficiently well-manned for strict control to be maintained, and viewed simply from the point of view of rearing the largest possible head of game, there was a good case to be made out for this policy. But with increased understanding of the fact that every creature of the countryside has a part to play, and that artificially eradicating one species from an area may rebound in unexpected ways on the very species meant to benefit, a greater tolerance is now evident. As a small example the old-time keeper waged a constant war against owls, when in practice the good they did by keeping down rats far exceeded the harm they caused among game bird chicks. The same reasoning can be applied to stoats and weasels, but one must be careful of making sweeping criticisms of the old-time keepers without considering the circumstances in which they lived and worked. If by good keepering they kept down the rats the usefulness of the natural predators of the rat vanished and, rats being scarce, the predators relied more on game for food. Additionally jobs were scarce in those times, and if a man's living depended upon plenty of pheasants and no vermin he wasted no time on ecological theories. Conservation makes good sense until its observance leaves a man hungry or poor. Try explaining to the sea fisherman in some areas around Britain that seals should enjoy complete protection.

The lesson to be learned from the past is that there is a balance to be struck between eliminating all predators and allowing them to flourish untouched, and the degree of interference must depend upon the nature of the shoot, and the extent to which you can exercise control. So far as hawks and owls are concerned the choice is out of our hands, for they are now all protected – and rightly so. In an area prone to rats I would be very reluctant to wage war too heavily on the stoats and weasels unless I had the time to control the rats myself. In practice stoats and weasels rarely offer the chance of a shot and I cover the subject of trapping in the next chapter. The rat is one of the very few creatures I dislike intensely, and which I would gladly see eliminated. My aversion is shared by the majority of mankind, and it is an interesting thought that those people who bitterly oppose blood sports are not found campaigning against the many cruel methods practised to kill rats. However, putting aside philosophy and coming down to the brass tacks of shooting rats, this is only really practical after dark for the rat is mainly a nocturnal animal. I have had great sport shooting them around farm buildings with a ·410 with a spot light taped under the barrel, but shooting makes no appreciable reduction, and poisoning is the only effective method for a large rat population. The exception is when the ground is firm enough to use a vehicle which can be driven down the hedgerows with the headlights on. By middle evening the rats will have moved out into the fields and great execution can be done as they dash back. The ideal vehicle is an open pick-up, part filled with straw bales against which you wedge your legs whilst firing over the cabin roof. The driver must proceed slowly, or the operation could be dangerous.

Crows, magpies, jays and to a lesser degree rooks, are all harmful to game and should be kept down within reason. The corvines have even sharper eyesight than a pigeon, and are considerably more wary. With an assistant to help, the jays and magpies can be driven through woods to a carefully placed Gun, and I deal with this practice in greater detail in the next chapter. Crows and rooks can be decoyed successfully to an owl decoy, but the best time for coming to terms with these two species is the spring. The crow can sometimes be shot in the nest, but usually it is necessary for two people to approach, one to walk away, and the other to hide and await the crow's return to the nest. The sport of shooting young rooks as 'branchers', that is when they have left the nest but are too young to fly any distance, is old established, and at one time rook rifles were made expressly for this purpose. The rook is considerably less harmful than the crow, and while it is sensible to prevent their numbers getting out of hand it would be a sorry day if the rook disappeared from the country scene. As a schoolboy during the war, when meat was scarce, I shot young rooks and later ate them as rook pie. As a dish I suspect I would have enjoyed it more had I not dealt with the preparation.

These, then, are the principal quarries found by the rough shooter. In their pursuit the observant man will learn a great deal not only about them but the countryside generally.

Chapter 12

KEEPERING AND REARING

Once you are successful in finding your own shoot your thoughts will soon turn towards increasing the stock of game it holds. The procedures of keepering and rearing are not arduous chores, but most interesting and great fun. The problem is time, for a full-time professional keeper has his hours fully occupied, and the amateur with probably only a few hours a week to spare must ensure that he gets his priorities right. There are two ways of increasing stock; firstly by improving habitat and eliminating hazards, and secondly by rearing birds. The newcomer tends to favour the latter approach, for it is very satisfying to rear and release stock, and the results are more obvious than the first process. Unfortunately this too often results in turning out inexperienced tender young birds in hostile surroundings overpopulated with predators, and the results of several months of hard work can be practically eliminated in a few days.

The first priority then is to improve the surroundings to give the game the best possible cover for shelter, breeding and food, and to reduce the numbers of harmful predators. An essential in this aim is to win the support of the farmer for there is much that he can do to make or mar the shoot. He can avoid, as far as possible, the use of poisonous sprays, report nests, try not to cut the hay until the partridges have hatched, leave the odd rough corner untouched, and even plant the occasional small area of game mixture for a nominal charge. However, you cannot gain the support of the farmer unless you earn it, and you must bear his interests in mind at all times. Apart from the obvious matters of shutting gates and leaving litter, you must control your dog, never shoot near or disturb stock, avoid even the least damage to crops; in fact every action must be weighed from the farmer's point of view. As an example I always let the farmer or keeper know I am around to save him the trouble of investigating if he hears a shot.

▲26   Crossing a small creek at low tide.
The gun is an under and over.

▼27   A wigeon retrieved at high tide.

28 Setting out duck decoys at low tide. As the tide makes the decoys will rise and show prominently.

The arrival of the barbed wire fence had enormous repercussions on wild life, for the subsequent disappearance of enormous lengths of hedges removed valuable cover. As a beginning therefore you should ensure that your ground has sufficient cover and if not do something about it. Clumps of hedge trimmings or gorse can be placed along wire fences, rough corners can be planted with thorn bushes or other suitable growth, and even the base of electricity pylons or power cable poles can be utilized.

It pays to make a big effort to reduce the predators before the nesting season begins, for the hen birds are at their most vulnerable then and subsequently the chicks are easy prey. If, without creating too much disturbance, you can find the whereabouts of nests it is often possible to protect them. A fertilizer bag, a shiny tin, or some similar 'human' object displayed a few yards from the nest will keep foxes away, and a strong smell, creosote or human urine, will have the same effect. Nests that are in danger from the feet of stock should be protected with a triangle of posts and wire, *after* obtaining the farmer's consent. Although some predator control can be done with a gun, traps have the advantage of costing very little and working 24 hours a day. The most effective trap is the tunnel where a spring trap is set in a short natural or artificial tunnel. This takes advantage of the natural tendency of stoats, weasels, rats, hedgehogs, etc., to explore any hole or tunnel. The trap should be of the humane type and suitable varieties can be seen advertised each week in the *Shooting Times* or *The Field*. Success depends mainly on siting the tunnels in the right places. Hedgerows are excellent as they form highways for hunting predators. In wide hedges or belts it helps to arrange some form of lead into the traps, and this can take the form of a wire netting fence, a fallen branch, or a furrow dug at an angle. The tunnel can be built of wood, stones, drainpipes, etc., and covered with turf. Alternatively natural tunnels in roots, under fallen trees, or similar situations can be used. An example of a good site is in a hedgerow on one side of a gate where predators, rapidly crossing the exposed ground, tend to dive into the first hole they find. New traps should be hung outdoors to allow the weather to erase the human smells before use. Once set they need a fine covering of dry soil. For humane reasons traps should be visited regularly.

Different predators will have a greater impact in different areas; for example in one spot foxes may be very troublesome yet twenty miles away non-existent. But taking the country as a whole the rat is the greatest enemy of game, and thereby deserves the amateur keeper's priority. Fortunately it is a relatively simple matter to poison them with Warfarin, laid in dry baiting points, and protected from stock and pets. Drainpipes are very suitable. It is essential that, once the rats begin feeding regularly on the poison, supplies are renewed daily until the local population is wiped out.

Fox destruction should be approached with discretion for if there is a local hunt you must consider their interests as well as your own. However, if this factor does not arise there is no question but that foxes are a major menace to game and should be kept down. Occasionally you may shoot a fox, and gassing earths with Cymag is another means of control, but the most effective method is snaring. Special heavy-duty snares should be purchased, and you must take great care to position them to avoid catching dogs or the legs of stock. Deer are also vulnerable but can be protected by placing a horizontal stick resting across two forked sticks about 18 inches above the ground and close to the snare. Deer will jump this, while foxes will pass underneath. As with other forms of traps snares should be visited at least daily. The loop should be about 8 inches long and 6 inches deep, and set about 5 inches above the ground. It should be supported by splitting a thin branch, wedging the wire in this, and pushing the opposite end of the branch into the ground. The opposite end of the snare needs very firmly anchoring, preferably to the trunk of a small tree.

Grey squirrels are best controlled in February or March, after the pheasant season is over, by poking out the dreys and shooting the occupants as they bolt. Crows and, where excessive in numbers, rooks, can be caught in cage traps. These are simply large open wooden frames of a box shape, and covered with wire netting. In the centre of the top is a hole opening into a funnel-shaped entrance which permits the bird to enter but not to fly up and leave again. The interior of the trap is baited with almost any food, but preferably something the birds recognize – hens' eggs, or a dead rabbit with the stomach opened. At first it is best to leave the roof off until the birds become used to feeding in the trap. Magpies and jays are very difficult to destroy, but can sometimes be shot successfully by driving a belt or wood to standing guns. This only works when the leaf is on the trees, and the standing Guns must stand on the fringe of the wood and not well back as for driven pheasant. Otherwise the relatively slow-flying jays and magpies will emerge slowly, spy the danger, and dart back into the wood. The nests of these two predators, and the crows, must be destroyed before the leaf bursts.

Hawks can be harmful to game, but are all protected by law. Even if they were not I would be very reluctant to destroy one.

Winter management is an important factor, for providing food and cover for game during the hard months not only attracts extra stock but ensures that the survivors enter the spring in good condition for breeding. An increasingly common practice is to plant patches of food-and-cover crops, which may include buckwheat, sunflowers, maize, kale and caraway. It is unnecessary to cover large areas – the object is to provide quiet small pockets preferably as sheltered as possible.

While food-and-cover crops are desirable winter feeding is practically essential. The system is to provide grain hoppers at suitable points which only require replenishing at intervals of several days, thereby eliminating the enormous time loss of hand feeding. Additionally a properly designed hopper prevents wastage through a host of other birds and animals dining uninvited. A typical hopper is a five gallon oil drum with a lid which overhangs to keep the contents dry, and vertical 4 inch slits around the base. If this is stood on a base which keeps it some 6 inches off the ground (two layers of bricks are suitable) then it is beyond the pecking reach of all the small birds. Game birds enjoy hunting for their food, and a layer of straw strewn over an open quiet spot in a wood will occupy them for hours. Whenever you visit the hoppers a few handfuls of grain should be tossed over the straw.

Having achieved the right environment the next step is to rear some birds for release. In the vast majority of cases this means pheasants, and provided you take care you should not only be successful but gain much pleasure and experience in the process. At the beginning you are faced with the age old problem of which comes first – the chicken or the egg. Professional keepers obtain their eggs by catching wild birds in 'fall traps' in February and placing them in laying pens. This will create various problems, and I would advise you to start by buying eggs from a game farm.

There is little more work involved in producing 100 pheasants than 50 so I suggest you aim at this figure. A skilled man would be content to put 100 poults into the woods from 150 eggs, so I suggest you buy 200. These can be hatched by incubator, but the hatching percentage is uncertain, and it would be very uneconomic to buy an incubator for this quantity. One alternative is to have them customed hatched, but this way you learn nothing, enjoy no pride of achievement and might just as well buy some day old chicks. This latter practice is a sure way of getting chicks, but as they have no natural mother you have to provide one in the form of a brooder which is a small hut with a source of heat. This can be bought or made and the whole subject is very thoroughly covered in the Game Conservancy's Booklet 8 *Pheasant Rearing* (25p). The Conservancy's address is Fordingbridge, Hampshire.

For the beginner the old method of hatching and rearing with broody hens is the simplest, cheapest, most rewarding, and, because the hen does the job, the method giving the fewest possibilities for disastrous mistakes. The first step – of finding the broodies – is the hardest. 16 pheasants' eggs can be hatched under a hen, and 12 to 14 under a bantam, but never put a newly acquired broody straight onto your precious game eggs; try her out on hens' eggs for two or three days. Any ordinary nest box will do, but for years I successfully hatched pheasants under a wide variety of boxes which had contained anything from oranges to beer. They must be waterproof and free from draughts, although some ventilation is important. The box should have no floor, and a saucer-shaped nest should be scraped in the ground and lined with hay. Every morning the broodies should be *very gently and quietly* lifted off, and tethered to a small stake while they eat and drink. In cold weather get them back as quickly as reasonably possible to avoid the eggs chilling – certainly in not more than 10 minutes, and meanwhile the box should be replaced over the eggs. In warm, dry weather flick drops of tepid water over the eggs to simulate natural dew. The eggs will hatch in about 24 days, and while the hen should be left in peace so far as possible you must watch for the occasional bird of murderous tendencies. These will kill their young as they hatch, and I always keep a spare broody on dummy eggs to take over a threatened clutch at short notice.

Leave the newly hatched chicks until they have all thoroughly dried then move them and the broody to the rearing pen. This is simply a wire netting covered run with a coop attached to one end. Plate 11 shows a rearing field with many runs. The hen is confined to the coop but the chicks can pass freely from run to coop. At the beginning the run can be small, say 4 feet by 3 feet, and 15 inches high, but it will need moving onto fresh ground daily. The ideal size of run in which to rear the birds to release would have a ground area of about 40 sq. ft., but this would be expensive, at least for a first step. Various temporary expedients will suggest themselves to the ingenious (I once reared 75 pheasants in a large fruit cage), but once you have mastered the technique of rearing it pays either to buy or build adequate pens. Whatever solution you adopt the chicks will grow rapidly and will soon need transferring into a larger pen.

For the first two or three nights the chicks should be shut in the coop to prevent their chilling, but they quickly learn to return to mother at dusk and the practice can be stopped. Feeding the chicks has descended from the highly secret formulas of the old keepers to the extremely simple procedure of buying a supply of pheasant chick crumbs and ensuring that the dishes are kept full. Fresh water is essential, and both this and the crumbs must be placed within reach of the broody. After six weeks the coops, broodies, and pheasant poults (as they have now become) are transferred to the woods. Not into dark, damp areas, but openings or clearings which enjoy sunshine and fresh air. The ideal time is late afternoon so the birds can spend the night in the coops, and have time to recover from the fright of the journey. Next morning the food and water should be positioned, the coop front released, and the poults should come out quietly. Now is the time that previous failure to deal with the predators will demand a heavy price. The coops and broodies can be left for some weeks. A professional keeper will keep his birds at home partly by feeding, and partly by dogging in the boundaries.

Unless you are in the rare position of having ample time you will find this impossible, so you must make do with feed hoppers and straw covered rides with grain. The important thing is to make your woods that much more attractive to the birds than anywhere else in the locality. It is interesting to ring your birds and see the percentage you shoot – 35 per cent or more is very good. Use a different colour or number for each year.

It is, of course, possible to buy poults of six to eight weeks, and simply turn them down, but apart from the fact that they will stray more you will have lost the fascination of transforming an egg into a strong free flying bird. As I wrote earlier in this book there is a very great deal more to shooting than firing a gun.

It is impossible to cover rearing and keepering in one chapter, and indeed it would be difficult to cover the subject fully in a complete book. However I do recommend the Game Conservancy's *Game on the Farm* (30p) which is a mine of information, and goes into far more detail than space has permitted me. Once again the address is Fording-bridge, Hampshire, and whilst writing I suggest you ask for details of the Conservancy. It deserves the support of all shooting men.

Chapter 13

PIGEON SHOOTING

The decimation of the rabbit population by myxomatosis has meant that the wood pigeon is now the most common quarry of the shooting man. On the ground it is, at least when viewed from a distance, a not very attractive plumpish bundle of grey feathers, although as Plate 22 shows the form and feathering improve at close quarters. But in the air it is a very different story for the woodie is fast and extremely keen eyed with an ability and inclination to change direction sharply which is not shared by the ducks and pheasants. It is impossible to drive pigeons as one would game birds, and their eyesight makes them most difficult to stalk. As a result making a decent bag of pigeons calls for far more fieldcraft and effort than merely standing at a peg and shooting driven pheasants, and many shooting men concentrate their efforts on what is a very worthwhile quarry.

The wood pigeon (*Columba p. palumbus*) is only one of several hundred species of pigeons and doves, and with the exception of some areas in the North and North West of Scotland it is found throughout Great Britain. Although it will nest in almost every month of the year the majority of the young that successfully leave the nest are hatched in August and September when the abundance of corn provides ample nourishment. By the end of September the pigeon population is at its peak for the year, and according to the studies of Dr. R. K. Murton winter losses will have reduced the numbers to approximately one half by the following spring. The pigeon has not only replaced the rabbit as the shooter's main quarry but also become the farmer's number one enemy. In the course of a year the grey hordes ravage a variety of crops, including peas, clover, sanfoin, newly-sown grain, and green crops; the latter suffering particularly in conditions of snow and frost when other food sources are either covered or frozen in. The capacity of the pigeon to damage crops and the enthusiasm of the shooting community to pursue it adds up to a situation of great harmony between sportsmen and farmers.

Pigeons can be shot in the late summer with two Guns walking up either side of a hedge and catching them as they slip off their nests. This is not exciting shooting, and although I appreciate the harm pigeons do to agriculture it is not a form of sport that attracts me. As both pigeons play a part in feeding squabs it may be that the survivor can support the young, but if it cannot they face a slow death.

If we eliminate the walking up we find that the three successful methods of shooting pigeons all depend on the fact that as you cannot easily go to the pigeons you must contrive matters so that the pigeons come to you. They are decoying, roost shooting, and flight line shooting, and we will consider them in that order.

DECOYING

Pigeons are gregarious birds, and tend to roost, fly and eat in flocks. As a result a flock of pigeons feeding on a crop acts like a magnet to other pigeons passing by, and this fact presents the pigeon shooter with the opportunity to bring birds in range by decoying. I will expand on the question of decoys shortly, but for the moment it is sufficient to explain that a decoy is any suitable material, usually rubber, plastic or tin, shaped and painted to resemble a pigeon. In the simplest possible terms decoying consists of laying out the decoys in a suitable spot, hiding within range and shooting the pigeons as they are lured in. This short sentence encompasses the wide range of skills, experience and fieldcraft which are called upon by the really successful pigeon shots who concentrate upon their sport with all the enthusiasm and dedication of the one species fisherman.

The novice to decoying usually makes his first mistake at the very beginning by decoying at what looks to be a suitable spot. Pigeons are very contrary birds and will show a preference for feeding in a particular part of a particular field which is apparently no different to a thousand other similar spots. In practice there will be a reason - the peas have speared a day or so earlier than elsewhere; the soil is lighter and is clogging their feet less; the drill went wrong and grain is lying on the surface - these, and a hundred other reasons can be the explanation; but at this stage in your pigeon shooting career the priority is to find the right spot first and worry about the reason later. Reconnaissance is the only answer, and not only on the day you shoot. In general decoying is more successful in the winter as the pigeons need more food to combat the cold, the daylight hours to feed are shorter, and the lesser number of suitable crops concentrates them into fewer fields. A careful watch on the summer and autumn farming programmes will tell you where to find the pigeons in the winter. Any stubble left unploughed will attract pigeons in the early winter, and will remain a draw until it has been cleared. Throughout the winter clover and lucerne will be the main source of food and when these are covered by snow the birds will switch to kale, sprouts, cabbage, and indeed any greenstuff that stands proud. Once the farmers start to sow the birds will switch with relish to cereals, peas and beans, moving on from field to field as the loose seeds on the surface are cleaned off. Other crops, wild as well as cultivated will attract but the man who knows his local countryside will have a good idea where to seek the pigeons. An hour spent slowly driving round observing the flight lines and the precise feeding areas of the birds is time very well spent.

Having determined where the pigeons want to feed the time has come to set up shop, and the uninitiated seeing the pigeon shooter staggering across a field with his load of equipment would not think this suggestion too far fetched. The first major need is the hide, and I could easily fill a chapter on the art of siting and building hides. The most flexible form is that built of straw bales arranged, when viewed as a plan, in a diamond shape with one end opened slightly to shoot through. This form has a bale roof, and provides excellent cover not only against sharp eyed pigeons but severe weather. It limits the angles over which one can fire, but if all is going well the birds will pass in front. The alternative form has an open roof, and allows the Gun to fire through 360 degrees. Concealment is harder in this hide, but when the birds are wilder it permits more shots.

The bale hide pre-supposes close co-operation with the farmer, which may not be so easy for the novice. The alternative is to build a hide from the materials available on the spot. I once had great fun shooting *down* onto incoming pigeons from the top of a straw stack, but in general the best place for a natural hide is in a hedge or on the edge of a wood. The materials are simple – a pocket knife and some string; the latter to tie back branches which once re-positioned form useful cover. There is little need to detail how to make a hide in a hedge, for trial and error will show the way in a few minutes. There are a few rules however. If the hedge has to contain stock do not weaken it. Before you cut the hole through which you will fire decide whether you will shoot sitting or standing. This may sound unimportant but it is wrong to move as a pigeon approaches. If, therefore, you are reluctant to spend some hours standing and intend to sit on a shooting stick or oil drum the hole needs cutting for this height. The hole should be no larger than is absolutely necessary. In winter the bare branches of the hedge will not give adequate cover, and will need to be supplemented with ivy leaves or camouflage netting. Unless the hedge is very thin the hide should be built in it rather than behind otherwise birds approaching from the rear will be alarmed. For the same reason overhead cover should be selected wherever possible.

The decoys should be set out some 20 to 25 yards from the hide, but not directly in front unless it is an absolutely still day. Remember that pigeons will always land into the wind, gliding in on set wings, and then flapping to break their forward speed, and sometimes dropping sharply in the last few feet. The right place to shoot them is not directly above the decoys when they are doing unpredictable things but a few yards previously as they glide on a straight path. Therefore, site the decoys slightly upwind of the hide so that the pigeons make the final stage of their glide into the wind when they are just opposite the gun. Avoid, if you possibly can, a hide/wind combination where the birds fly straight towards you – they are too likely to spot you. The converse where the pigeons come in over the top of the hide is also bad as you have insufficient warning of their approach. The decoys should face head into wind but not all at the same angle like soldiers. Watch the behaviour of a feeding flock and you will see that short of actually turning their backs to the wind they adopt every angle. I favour a pattern of decoys shaped like a crescent, pointing into the wind, with the density of birds increasing towards the centre. The effect of this is to encourage pigeons to land just behind the thickest central concentration which has been positioned so that the incoming birds are the ideal distance from the gun. Decoys should be positioned to be as prominent as possible, either by positioning them on clumps of earth, or cutting down the surrounding growth. In the Plate 20 it can be seen that the stubble has been roto-scythed down to permit the decoys to show up. This photo is also a good illustration of pigeon decoying from a bale hide.

With the decoys in position the shooter now retires to the hide and waits. Decoying shares with marriage the fascination of being somewhat unpredictable, for the results are not necessarily what the preliminary research and planning have suggested. There are days when the pigeons come in non-stop and the sport is a blur of load, fire, reload, look round for the next and fire again. There are others when an hour will be passed observing a pair of partridges on the headland, and hoping the old crow calling from the wood will fly over. On more than one occasion I have given thanks for the opportunity to let off a barrel at a passing starling. Given normal luck, however, there will be a reasonable degree of movement with pigeons passing to and fro. For three years I kept a careful record of the weather conditions on every day I decoyed to see what, if any, difference specific variations made to pigeon movement. (Obviously the more pigeons move about the more likely they are to spot and be attracted to the decoys.) Minor trends could be discerned with temperature variation, cloud cover, etc., but one major fact stoood out - wind makes pigeons move. Why I have yet to decide, for one would expect that movement was harder and more boisterous in a wind. Perhaps the pigeons actually enjoy flying in wind, but whatever the reason they are unquestionably more active on windy days than still.

Let us return, however, to the hide. In due course a passing pigeon will pause in its flight, veer, and head for the decoys. The art at this instant is to eliminate all unnecessary movement. Your head should be behind a thin screen of twigs or dead grass, not directly exposed. Through this the eye can watch closely while the hands gently ease the barrels into position. If the preliminary work has been well done the body will already be in position; and as the pigeon makes the final run-in the butt comes to the shoulder, the head rises slightly, and the pigeon dies without ever knowing danger was near.

Do not rush out of the hide. Sink back and wait, for the report could have put up other pigeons in the vicinity which may soon come in. During 'hot' periods dead pigeons can be left strewn around the decoys in all attitudes without alarming new arrivals. Eventually there will be a dull patch and dead birds can be set up to supplement the existing decoys. The bigger the flock of decoys the better their pulling power. 30 decoys may draw a passing flock of 20 which might have ignored a dozen decoys. I never start with less than 10 decoys, and only stop setting up dead birds when I have 75 or so. After this the area covered is so great that the pigeons may settle too far from the hide. To set birds up sharpen a stout twig at both ends, push one end up through the crop and neck of the pigeon into the skull and the other end into the ground. Only a third or thereabouts should be treated this way for this is a position of alertness, and while the head up attitude makes the decoys more obvious the majority should be feeding. This can be achieved by just pushing the beak into the ground. If several birds come in together let one settle and take the first shot at one in the air. As the first bird has then to take off it will present an easier target for your second barrel than one which was airborne when the alarm sounded. Of course if your aim is killing pigeons rather than sport let several settle and shoot the first on the ground. It is good sense to use a lighter load cartridge than normal as the birds are usually near and easily killed and the cramped position makes it harder to absorb recoil.

Some years ago decoys were either entirely artificial or made by preserving the real thing. Obviously the finest imitation of a pigeon is a dead pigeon, but this involved opening the bird, removing the breast and innards, stuffing the cavities with cotton wool, and sewing up the skin. Whilst staying with a keen ornothologist friend he showed me some wings of birds which he used whilst lecturing, and I asked how he preserved them. 'Formalyn', was the answer, and for the next twelve months I experimented. In 1965 *The Field* published the results, in the form of an article recommending the use as decoys of whole pigeons preserved with Formalyn, and this method of decoy making is becoming increasingly popular. So it should when one considers that it costs about a new penny as against the 75p or thereabouts of the artificial decoy and does a better job. The requirements, all from the local chemist are a large bore hypodermic syringe and a bottle of Formalyn. A dead pigeon is liberally injected, not only in the main body, but in the fleshy parts of the wings, legs, and neck. It should then be laid, with the head propped in whichever position you wish, in an outhouse or garage (Formalyn smells) and left for some weeks. In this time the body dehydrates, and you are left with a light, tough and most lifelike decoy, which, when the feathers become too scruffy, can be replaced at negligible cost. They are best carried in the small polythene bags intended for sandwiches.

Any Formalyn which touches the skin should be washed off at once with cold water. Great care should be taken to keep it out of the eyes.

As I wrote at the start of this chapter the subject of successfully decoying pigeons is complex and I have only been able to cover it in bare detail. There are several good books on pigeon shooting, but I would recommend *Pigeon Shooting* by Archie Coats, published by André Deutsch.

ROOST SHOOTING

Although the sport is condensed into a shorter space of time, usually the last two hours of light, I prefer roost shooting to decoying as the pigeons offer a much greater variety of shots and are mostly more difficult. In fact I once wrote in *The Field* that if the medical world gave me one last hour's shooting I would be sorely tempted to spend it roost flighting pigeons. I went on 'I would not squander this last nostalgic hour on any ordinary day, but would wait for a cruel evening when a cold wind roared through the tree tops and it was a toss up whether it would rain or snow before dawn. It would be one of those glorious nights when the pigeons poured in like a never ending grey river, and in a frenzy of spotting, firing, loading and picking up, to the wild sound of the bustling wind, slapping branches and roar of the gun, the mind would grow bemused by the speed of events and later recall the evening just as a wild exciting jumble'. Which just about sums up roost shooting at its best.

Roost shooting is mainly a winter occupation, partly because the absence of leaves makes it possible to see the pigeons, and partly because the cold weather discourages them from roosting anywhere but in the larger warmer woods. Results are best in those areas where arable farming encourages a large pigeon population but where suitable roosting woods are scarce. The ideal is a pheasant covert, in such countryside, which has been kept quiet throughout the rearing and shooting seasons with the result that the pigeons drop in confidently. When roost shooting starts immediately after pheasant shooting ends the bag for the first few nights is usually very good. Windy nights, particularly in severe weather, are best, and still ones are worst. In many areas a given night each week is designated for roost shooting, and every wood throughout one large area is manned. This keeps the birds moving from wood to wood and greatly increases the sport.

The most frequent mistake committed by both experienced Guns and beginners is to shoot when the birds are too high. Quite frequently, and particularly on still nights or when they have been much shot, the pigeons will circle warily. If you remain still, and keep your face down, they will drop in. Most newcomers are bothered by the canopy of branches, and try to shoot the pigeons through any clear gaps that exist. This is quite unneccessary and only complicates an already tricky shot. The secret is to completely ignore the overhead cover and shoot normally. Unless you hit a large branch the loss of pellets from obstructions will be insignificant. Although the main flight will probably not last more than half an hour it is well worth being in position at least two hours before dark. There will probably be a useful trickle of targets from this time on, and, equally important, they will enable you to establish where the main flight will try to roost and its line of approach. Pigeons will always make their final landing run into the wind, and after the shot the remainder will fling sideways and dash off down wind.

There is no need for an elaborate hide, and once the light begins to fade it is quite sufficient to stand with your back to a tree, always provided that you keep still. The greater need is to pick a spot where there is a high canopy of thin overhead branches. This way the birds are obvious to you, but the pigeons looking down at a maze of branches rushing by beneath them can see very little through it. As with decoying, when a flock of pigeons drop in the nearest should be left for the second barrel.

Some roost shooters favour setting decoys in the trees to encourage the pigeons to drop in. I have experimented with these, but while I have found them useful on occasions my view is that the bother of placing and subsequently removing them is greater than the possible gain. Decoys will not bring birds into a wood to which they would not otherwise have come. They will bring pigeons in with more confidence, and possibly vary the part of the wood they roost in. But these two advantages are rather minor for if you conceal yourself they will come in in the end, and it is easier to move to the spot the pigeons favour than to try to attract them to you. Picking up the slain is a problem, for moving about on this task will scare off many incoming birds. Personally I let them lie when the pigeons are active, and pick up as rapidly as possible in the slack periods. If you are attempting to cover a large wood single handed the pigeons will eventually drop into the areas you cannot see and thereafter attract other incoming birds. A useful remedy is to put up one or more of the 'crow scarer' ropes of bangers which explode every fifteen minutes or so. Carefully placed these will not only put off the cunning ones, but drive them over you. Never be in a hurry to leave. As the light fades movement may fall off until you feel the birds have all gone to roost elsewhere, but if they really favour your wood they will sometimes make a last attempt before nightfall. In this they can be near suicidal, and provide some of the best sport of the flight.

FLIGHT LINE SHOOTING

Flight line shooting is rarely premeditated, but usually an act of initiative taken when conditions create a strong movement of pigeons along a specific route. Every experienced pigeon shot will know the established flight lines for his area, but they are not used every day. A line will come in or out of use according to varying conditions of food supplies or weather. A newly sown field of spring wheat may open up a flight line from the roosting woods, and dry up a line to some distant clover fields. Or a gale-force wind may concentrate all pigeon movement in an area under the shelter of a belt of trees. It is rarely worthwhile setting out with the specific intention of shooting a flight line; the need is to keep an eye open for a line developing and to take advantage of it. The flight may die out after only an hour or so, but while it lasts it can give enormous sport. Obviously some form of hide is necessary but this need not be elaborate, and can be built very quickly.

There are several general tips which apply to all forms of pigeon shooting. Number 6 shot, and standard loads, are perfectly adequate for pigeons. The old fashioned idea that heavy loads and magnum guns were necessary was nonsense. When decoying or roost shooting always take plenty of cartridges. You may not even fire a box full, but it is a pity to run out when conditions are good. A plastic sack weighs very little, can be useful to sit on or form a waterproof roof for a hide, and on the good days solves the problem of carrying the bag. I still remember carrying 122 pigeons from a bale hide in the centre of a vast Cambridgeshire field to the car some quarter of a mile away with a standard game bag and a couple of yards of string. When it comes to cooking pigeons a great deal of work produces a vast amount of feathers but very little meat. The simplest method is to run a sharp knife along the breast bone, pull back the skin and slice off the breast meat. In this way you will get more than three quarters of the meat in a tenth of the time. There is more on the subject of pigeon cookery in Chapter 19.

29   Mallard rising.

30 Leaving a salt water marsh after a very successful flight. The wildfowler will have his topcoat in the rucksack to avoid getting too hot.

Chapter 14

WILDFOWLING

Many people mistakenly believe wildfowling to be simply the pursuit of ducks and geese, which is wrong, for the quarry of the true wildfowler not only includes certain waders but, more important, it is sought in a restricted area. The hunting grounds of the wildfowler are below the high water mark of the tides in the strange and wonderful world that varies from the vast eerie mud flats of the Wash to the harsh rocks of the Hebrides, and over which the tides sometimes creep and sometimes roar twice each day. Above this mark the sport is not wildfowling but duck shooting, whether it is flighting wigeon on a fresh water marsh or mallard on corn stubble.

The mental picture conjured up by the thought of a wildfowler is romantic. One visualizes a man knowledgeable in the ways of the sea and the fowl, revelling in the challenge and atmosphere of his wild and desolate surroundings, and gathering a modest harvest of his quarry. Reality is usually very different. The wildfowler is frequently cold, often wet, and sometimes bored. The truth is that the majority of men that try their hand at the sport give up within a season or so, and some of those that persevere do so because they have no alternative shooting. What then is the motive that drives on the hard core of enthusiasts to go out in all weathers, invariably to experience discomfort, sometimes to face danger, usually to return empty-handed?

There is no simple answer, but I believe the truth is woven with several strands, the strength of which will vary from man to man. Unquestionably the environment will appeal to those who have a love of wild, desolate, open places in which the wide range of the temper of the weather has full play. There is no dawn to better the fiery red glow of an angry sunrise on the Wash, reflected across the miles of glittering mud or sand; and there is no gale more awe inspiring than one that has bred in the open vastness of the Atlantic before striking the West coast of Scotland with an anger that makes the very rocks tremble. I believe that as man and his artificially created surroundings become more sophisticated – as he becomes ever more cushioned from nature – so in the more manly man, if you take my point, there grows a desire to be back to nature once more. To feel the pull of the mud on aching legs; to lie close with the ground and smell the marsh grasses and the salt, and sense the cruel fingers of an East wind creeping through to the bones. This is hunting in the full sense – hunting as our forefathers hunted centuries ago with all the odds on the quarry and success depending on tenacity, fieldcraft and a slice of luck. The men who become and remain wildfowlers are the type of men a country depends on in time of war. Wildfowling strips the veneer of civilization from a man, and sends him back to the concrete and neon lights with a feeling that for all this he is still an independent being who can look after himself. There is a fascination too about the quarry that can never be attached to a pheasant which hatched in the next field. As I lift a wigeon from the mud I marvel at the romance that attaches to a bird which has bred thousands of miles to the North in a spot which is now gripped in the frost of an Arctic winter. And no shooting man hears the call of the wild geese without a shiver of excitement.

Wildfowling then is an arduous sport beset with discomfort and disappointment. I will assume you have not been ruined by our so called advanced society, and proceed to tell you how to set about it.

As with all shooting the first problem is to find somewhere to shoot. There are still people who believe that the shooting below the high water mark is free for all but this is quite untrue: as I explained in Chapter 2, the majority belongs to the Crown and the remainder is privately owned. In those areas where fowl are prolific, or where the proximity of large towns has caused heavy shooting pressure, the local wildfowling clubs have almost invariably negotiated some form of lease and shooting is restricted. Later in this chapter I warn against fowling except in the company of an experienced friend, and if you have such a human gem he will already have a venue. If not I urge you to join WAGBI (Grosvenor House, 104 Watergate Street, Chester) and obtain from them the address of your nearest wildfowling club. Join this; attend the meetings, put something into the club, be it helping at clay shoots or addressing envelopes for the secretary, and in time the club will help you over where to shoot. If you can afford it the easiest, safest and most effective method is to contact one of the professional guides who advertise in the *Shooting Times* or *The Field*.

I realize that this advice is no sure guideline to shooting but I can do no more. If you have the qualities necessary to make a wildfowler you will certainly find the ground.

A wildfowler's dress must be practical, which means it must be inconspicuous and keep you dry and warm. Browns and greens are the best colours, but normal shooting clothing is rarely man enough for the job for it must be capable of keeping out the wet even when you are lying in the mud. Technology has brought many new fibres but I have yet to find anything to beat the 'Solway' smock made by Barbours of South Shields. It is heavy and stiffens when wet, but it is really waterproof and almost untearable. All the advice I gave in Chapter 10 about clothing applies, but more so, for keeping warm on a salt marsh in hard weather calls for maximum protection. The other departure from dress for the land is the absolute need for waders which are essential, not only for crossing creeks and gutters but kneeling. When trying on waders for size allow extra room for thick socks, but not too much for loosely fitting waders will pull off in thick mud. I wear a pair of old waterproof over-trousers cut off above the knee which allows me to sit on the mud without getting a wet behind. The jacket must have a hood. Given this outfit it is possible to sit out the worst of storms and remain dry (if not warm). Most gunsmiths sell the small hand warmers which burn lighter fuel, and in cold weather these are a godsend. Many times it is only these devices which have kept my trigger finger supple.

You will quickly find that the clothing necessary to keep you warm on the marsh when you are stationary will cause you to sweat when walking any distance. Equally if you dress for walking in comfort you will soon grow cold when you stop. The remedy is to carry part of your clothing and don it immediately you stop – not when you have grown cold. In addition to this you will have other items of equipment, and all this is best carried in a rucksack which sets the weight high on the back. The ordinary game bag drags on one shoulder, and settles the weight too low. Remember that anything you take on a marsh will suffer badly from mud, wet and salt, and while your equipment should be sound it should not be expensive. I frequently carry a wading pole, which in my case is a fancy name for a broom stick. This is useful to test the depth of mud and water before entering; as a third leg whilst climbing muddy banks; and laid across two pyramids of mud with grasses dangled from it forms the basis of a hide. Every wildfowler has his own peculiar items of equipment, but a compass should be standard for all. Never go on the marsh without it – it might save your life. A whistle might do the same if you were lost in fog with a rising tide. Many fowlers carry binoculars not only to observe their quarry but the many other birds of the sea shore. I always carry a square of the thin black polythene sheet used by builders as a waterproof membrane. This weighs almost nothing, folds into the smallest corner, and can be lain on for hours without letting the damp through. A flask of hot soup or coffee is well worth the price of its weight. Experience will suggest other items in time, but it will quickly become obvious to the novice that a good dog is essential if the successful shots are to be bagged. All too often the bird will fall across a deep creek or in the sea, and whilst I have swum in the North Sea in mid winter on more than one occasion the novelty soon wears off. It is not so much the shock of the water that palls, as the experience of standing naked on the tide edge in several inches of mud pulling dry clothes onto a wet blue body.

Most fowlers go through the stage of believing that the solution to knocking down those elusive ducks and geese is a larger more powerful gun with an increased range. As I explained in Chapter 5, this is largely a fallacy, for the disadvantage of the extra weight is considerable, both in carrying and aiming the weapon, and the extra range gained is small. However there is a lot of pleasure to be had from experimenting and you may well wish to try alternative guns. In due course though you may reason that if a top tennis player or cricketer strives to ensure that his racquets or bats are always identical in weight and balance then it is crazy for you to shoot with a $6\frac{1}{2}$ lb 28 inch 12 bore at pigeons one day, and with an $8\frac{1}{2}$ lb 30 inch 10 bore at duck the next. Personally I use for wildfowling a gun which is as near as possible an exact, but cheaper, replica of my standard 12 bore. In practice the beginner is unlikely to buy a gun specially for fowling, and unless you take care the salt and sand will do horrible things to your doubtless valued gun. At least in the early days you will be wise to carry it in a sleeve slung over your back. This protects the gun, leaves your arms free, and is safer. It will give very considerable protection if you spray the gun just before you go on the marsh, and immediately you come off, with one of the gun oils specifically designed to combat wet and rust. Naturally the gun should never be laid on the mud or sand, and every effort should be made to keep the moving parts fr ee of grit. If you fall, stumble, or get stuck always check afterwards that the barrels are not blocked with mud.

Many lengthy books have been written about wildfowling, all of them choked with practical information and to convey this wealth of knowledge in a few paragraphs is impossible. The latest, and far and away the best of these tomes, is *The New Wildfowler in the 1970's*, which is WAGBI's own publication. But whatever you read one fact should stand out – that the tide is of paramount importance. No fowler would enter a marsh without knowing the state of the tide, for not only does this influence the movement of the fowl but his very life depends upon it. The tide flows and ebbs twice in each twenty-four hours, and the heights to which it rises and falls are not constant but vary as the moon varies its position to the earth. Full and new moons produce the spring tides which have the maximum rise and fall, and the quarter and half moons the neap tides which have the minimum. A tide table will predict the times and heights of the tides for a given area, but you must appreciate that these are only predictions and severe gales can alter both times and depth, sometimes to a dangerous degree.

At this stage I would make most forcibly the point that wildfowling is a dangerous sport, and it is a rare year in which some fowlers are not drowned. Experienced men are caught out occasionally, but the vast majority of these unfortunates are novices who have simply not comprehended the dangers. You *must* not go wildfowling without an experienced companion. Death nearly always comes because the fowler is trapped by the rising tide, having failed to leave the low ground in time. He may have misread his tide table; become too engrossed in shooting and failed to see the grey fingers stealing up the creeks; become lost in a fog; caught by nightfall; or stuck in the mud, but in the end it is the water that gets him. I once struggled off the Wash in the pitch dark, a long way from where I thought I was, saturated, and very frightened, and I know how easy it is to underestimate the sea. It is a killer, and you must treat it as such.

The art of wildfowling is getting within range of the fowl. The more experienced a fowler you become the more forcibly will the truth of this simple statement hit you. It is just not possible to set down in words a formula for solving this problem for every area has its own difficulties and solutions, and in turn these vary from day to day. All I can do is to set down the problems you will have to overcome, and the circumstances that will help you. The game is played in such open flat surroundings that it will rarely be possible for you to go to the fowl – you will have to intercept them as they move, and this means a knowledge of where and when they move and why. The major movements of wildfowl occur at dawn and dusk, and also with changes of the tide. Although there are exceptions in general terms duck feed at night and rest during the day, and geese do the reverse. It is the movement from the roosting to the feeding areas and vice versa that triggers off the enormous and exciting movement of fowl each dawn and dusk. The birds do not move aimlessly, but follow flight lines which vary with the feeding and roosting grounds, the weather and the tide. No punter, pouring over the latest form reports, ever had half the fun of a wildfowler calculating where to stand for the forthcoming flight. The reasoning might well follow these lines, 'At dawn the geese will come to the chapped potatoes on the big field by the black barn. At dusk they flew off to roost on the North bank, but the tide will have floated them off at 3 a.m. By dawn they should have drifted to opposite the main sluice, but the cloud is thick which means they won't lift until late, and when they do the wind from the South West will push them further North. Therefore I must lie at least 400 yards along the wall from the sluice.'

The behaviour of wildfowl varies from area to area; for example in a remote part of Scotland where they are never shot, duck will flight in to feed well before dusk, but in hard shot areas it will often be practically dark before they move. Some circumstances are common everywhere. Strong winds are the wildfowlers' greatest ally for they force the quarry to fly low. On nights when there will be no moon the duck must flight before it is dark, but if there will be a bright moon they may well ignore dusk, and wait for it. Contrary to the beginners usual expectation fowl can be more easily seen against a background of thin cloud than a clear sky. The very earliest you should give up is when it is too dark to see your feet. As a general rule teal flight before mallard and wigeon. At dusk it is more important to pick up shot fowl immediately than at dawn; in the latter case the light is improving all the time. When, at dusk, the light is still strong it is necessary to lie down or hide in a creek, but as it dims you can stand provided you keep quite still. If there is little or no wind, and you keep still, you will hear the wings of duck long before you see them. Once it is fairly dark duck are always nearer than they appear. If the sea is rough and the tide full so that the duck cannot roost on mud or sand they will flight earlier than if it is quiet. Given really rough conditions duck will move inland during the day for shelter. At low tide it often pays to investigate the creeks in the hope of finding small parties of duck which can be stalked. Apart from this activity the man who is moving rarely shoots anything. Movement in the wide open areas of a marsh is very obvious and you must pick your spot and hide up. The most comfortable places are the shallow gutters where they join a creek. It nearly always pays to wait near the more major water channels as these are frequently followed by the fowl when they move at low tide.

Apart from dawn and dusk the greatest movement of the wildfowl, and therefore the best chance of sport, occurs as the tide makes, forcing the fowl to move off their roosting areas. In fact the degree of movement is such that the birds often appear to be flying for the sheer pleasure of it, covering considerably more distance than is necessary, often at high speeds. A marsh is a fascinating sight as the tide makes, gradually drowning first the mud and then the grasses, with more and more waves of ducks and waders lifting into the air and charging to and fro until the sky is filled with armies of birds all, by some natural miracle, wheeling and diving as one with their pack. The problem for the fowler is that the birds tend to fly along the edge of the rising tide, and as fast as you settle into a good position so the tide drives you out again. The most effective form of tide flighting is to find a high point which will not be covered by the tide, and put out decoys some 15 to 25 yards away. These will lie on the surrounding mud or grass, and as the tide lifts them may attract other duck. Make sure they are well secured to a peg or heavy weight, and study the natural formation of duck on the water to see how to arrange them.

The two most important aspects of concealment are dress, and keeping still. At the beginning of the season the thick growth of marsh grasses provide ample cover just by lying down, but as the winter frosts scythe down the growth the fowlers tend to retreat into the gutters and creeks which provide good cover, although not always where one wants it. Scraping a shallow 'grave' in sand or mud, and building the excavated material into a small wall on the side you expect the fowl is effective but a bad shooting position. Kneeling in a gutter is better. A roll of wire netting and several canes form the basis of an excellent hide which is completed by weaving grasses through the wire. I once built a hide of miniature ice floes in a very hard winter, on the Medway. But whatever your hide avoid making it too high and conspicuous. Prominent lumps in an otherwise flat marsh alarm birds.

Shooting is often difficult for the wildfowler, for he is frequently standing in deep mud and unable to move his feet, kneeling, or even lying on his back. The lack of obvious features makes it difficult to judge range, and a common fault of the novice is to fire at birds out of range.

Correct behaviour on the marsh is mainly common sense. Keep well away from other wildfowlers, and avoid unnecessary movement once they have taken up their positions. Do not shout to companions, or flash torches. If you see birds approaching the hiding points of others keep still and quiet. Never fire at a bird unless you are certain it is a legitimate quarry, and then never do so unless it is clearly within range. WAGBI publish an excellent booklet, *Know Your Quarry*, which will be a great help in identification.

Duck should not be hung for long; personally, a couple of days is long enough for me. Their taste varies with their food, as you will discover if you eat a mallard in September which has lived off corn stubbles and later another which has existed on a salt marsh throughout a hard January. Young teal are quite superb eating.

Chapter 15

DUCK SHOOTING INLAND

As I explained in the last chapter, true wildfowling takes place below the sea wall, and the wildfowler is inclined to look down on the inland duck shooter as a man whose sport calls for less endurance. This is sometimes unfair, for the wildfowler tucked cosily in a creek as a cruel east wind screams overhead is much better off than the gunner only a few hundred yards away over the sea wall with no cover but a yard of camouflage net hung over a barbed wire fence. One of the fascinations of inland duck shooting is the great variety of settings it embraces for one week you can be flighting mallard into a gravel pit on the edge of a city and the next walking a remote reed fringed Scottish loch for teal. Practically all inland waters are visited by duck at one time or another, and these range from large areas of water; some natural like the English Lake District, and some artificial like reservoirs, to small farm ponds. The former will hold duck, although in varying numbers, the year through, whereas the latter may only be visited when, for example, an overhanging oak drops its acorn crop.

As a sport it has much of the fascination of wildfowling with the challenge of outwitting a free flying quarry, but without some of the discomforts. Before dealing with the problems and possible solutions I will briefly touch on geese. I have deliberately not headed this chapter 'Wildfowl shooting Inland' because while it is not illegal to shoot geese inland it is generally regarded as bad practice to shoot them on their feeding grounds. While the various species of geese exist in greater numbers than the uninformed appreciate they survive in a world where many pressures are stacked against them. They are sensitive to disturbance (as witness the departure of the large numbers which once wintered on the North Norfolk coast before over-shooting drove them away) and should be allowed to roost and feed unmolested.

As with wildfowling the crux of the matter is getting within range of the duck. In most cases the only hope is to anticipate the duck's movements and lie in wait, but on occasions it is possible to approach within range of stationary duck. I have happy memories of taking a pair of mallard from a stubble field on the Isle of Skye by slithering up the furrows of a potato field, but the opportunities usually occur on water. Walking a river bank will often produce a shot, particularly where it winds and shields you from view. On straight rivers it is necessary to walk in large loops, touching the bank at intervals, and trying to spot duck in the distance before they spot you. If you are successful take great care to pick out some natural feature to mark their precise location. Surroundings look very different when viewed from a new angle, and an error of a few yards can make the difference between a shot and a quarry just out of range. Walking the edge of reed-fringed lakes or lochs can give good sport, but it is essential to walk at the very edge or the ducks will sit tight. When teal are disturbed out of range it pays to take cover, or, if there is none, lie flat, for they will often circle and present a chance. The sheltered areas of small inland waters near the sea are well worth a visit in rough weather as they provide shelter for coastal duck. Another method of approaching duck has given me great sport, although it can only be classed as inland duck shooting by the narrowest margin. Along the steep and rocky coastlines it is common to find pools of rainwater above the high water mark which, although brackish from the salt water spray, are essentially fresh and therefore attractive to the duck of the shore. This is particularly so in gale conditions when the large surrounding rocks not only give shelter from the buffeting wind but cover to the gunner. I have spent many hours in this pursuit along various Hebridean coastlines and enjoyed a rare combination of scenery and sea smells, sounds and breezes. It is often rather dangerous for the rocks are frequently covered by wet slippery seaweed.

From time to time other opportunities will occur for surprising stationary duck, and doubtless you will seize them, but the real cream of inland duck shooting lies in ambushing the quarry. Ideally a duck should die without ever having realized danger was near. The secret of forecasting the movements of duck is to know where they feed and where they shelter, and to intercept them en route. Usually success is more easily found at dusk than dawn, for at dusk they are dropping into their feeding areas which are generally more concentrated than their resting areas. As an example I have shot many duck in Skye flighting into the small patches of oats grown by the crofters. Lying on the fringe, among the thistles and the sweet grasses, it is almost impossible not to be within range. But at dawn when the duck return to the vast sea lochs the chance of hitting the flight line is remote. Sometimes, of course, the resting area will be small, possibly only a pond, but in this event I would urge you not to shoot it. Duck disturbed at their feeding grounds will simply find another larder, but if their rest areas are shot they will leave the area. In practice you may not have access to either area, which means that you must find the flight line between the two. This is the more easily done the nearer you are to the point of take off or landing. Remember duck have an affinity with water and will follow a river whenever it leads them in approximately the right direction. The pattern of duck behaviour, not only in their flight lines, but the fields and waters they favour remains constant year after year and the wise man will take a modest harvest but avoid shooting so hard that the pattern is ruined.

Discovering the day resting areas is often a simple matter of scanning the sea or large inland waters with binoculars, but finding the feeding grounds can be most difficult. The fact that by the time the birds flight it is often so dark that visibility is down to a few yards intensifies the problem. Assuming you enjoy the right to look for them over a wide area the best course is to search during the day for signs of the night visitors. These are signs of feeding, for example laid corn with the ears cropped, feathers, and, on land, droppings. The latter can be the most helpful of all, for droppings can show not only that duck have been there but when. As the droppings age so they both dry, lose colour, and slightly flatten. Many droppings a few of which are coloured, damp and round, tell that a few duck have been using the area for a long time. Conversely many mainly new droppings mean many duck for a short time. No matter how many droppings there may be it is pointless flighting the spot if none of them are new. The duck may have eaten all the acorns or whatever other food had attracted them, or been shot at, but if they have abandoned the place it is pointless to waste time. There are traps for the amateur sleuth. Damp droppings which, when broken, are dry in the centre are merely old droppings which have been briefly rained on. Old droppings which have been saturated by rain can be detected for the frauds they are by their lack of colour and loss of shape. Fresh feathers are a good guide, but on water must be sought on the shore to which the winds of the last few days will have driven them. This is not necessarily the shore on which the duck feed. Fresh cartridge cases prove that duck have been around, but may also show that they have left for good. Always pocket your cases, and toss them well out into the water. There is no point in publicizing your knowledge. On the other hand there is much harmless fun to be had by dropping your empty cases at a suitable spot later. The simplest, and therefore the least satisfying, method of intercepting duck is the fed flight pond. This is a small area of water which is regularly baited with any food favoured by duck. This can be corn, acorns, rotting apples, old potatoes, over ripe bananas, or any other food their catholic tastes embrace. Sensibly used such a pond can give good sport, but there are people who through a combination of greed and utter indifference to the needs of sensible conservation make very large bags. Usually flight ponds are well provided with butts giving not only cover but shelter from the weather, and it is the size of the bag and the relative luxury of the conditions which stimulate the criticism of the wildfowlers who often endure severe conditions for no bag at all. In flight pond shooting the results are entirely dependant on the number of ducks using the pond, and it is a test of marksmanship rather than fieldcraft. In my view there is a heavy moral obligation on flight pond shooters to rear at least as many duck as they shoot.

Intercepting duck under natural conditions is a totally different matter, calling not only for the obvious skills but a slice of luck as well. So many little factors can alter the behaviour of duck, and if you discover what appears to be heavily used ground, flight it as soon as possible – tomorrow may be too late. Food is the main attraction of an area for duck, although near the coast shelter and fresh water offer additional attractions for the duck on the sea. Two personal examples will illustrate typical situations. For some years I rented a fresh water marsh actually adjoining the sea wall in North Kent. Each winter much of the ground would flood, but only to the depth of an inch or so. Then, at dusk, the wigeon would flight in, sometimes in their hundreds, to graze. At the other end of the country I have had many blissful hours in settings of such beauty as to be almost unearthly. Where the stark hills of the Hebrides flatten out to meet the Atlantic the coasts are dotted with little crofts, each growing a patch of oats. Into these the mallard and teal drop at dusk, silhouetted like great moths against the deep blue expanse of the Western sky. In the evenings of early Septembers, I have lain among the wild flowers and the grasses, watching for the first flicker of wings over the sea, while the last rays of the sun have painted the tips of the Cuillin Hills pink. A heron will flap along the shore; a curlew's bubbling liquid call flows in from the estuary; overhead a snipe will drum; and whether the duck have come or not I have enjoyed a rare tranquillity.

I permit myself to romance in this fashion from time to time simply to remind you that shooting has many more considerations than the successful pursuit of wild creatures. The test of a day is not the number of cartridges fired and the bodies in the game bag, but the extent to which you enjoyed it.

Assuming that you have, by a combination of common sense and observations, correctly forecast the movements of the duck, the extent to which you benefit from your knowledge will depend upon sensible positioning and concealment. Sometimes the one will determine the other; for example where there is a dyke offering the only cover, but where you have a choice several points need taking into account. Firstly always remember that the duck will approach their feeding grounds into the wind – if you are upwind they will land before they reach you. Next arrange your position so that you can fire before they drop below the horizon, for they may then be invisible. It is best to be in a position to shoot as the birds are making the last few yards of their approach and not when they are directly over the feeding area, for this way they are not only reasonably above the skyline but their flight is steady. Finally try to position yourself so they pass between you and the Western sky where the light will be strongest and they will present the best silhouette.

In the closing stages of the flight it will be permissible to stand provided you keep still, but at the beginning some form of hide is important. In laid corn it will be sufficient to lie on the fringe, or if it has been combined, a low hide can be quickly made of straw rakings. Most ponds and lakes will have cover round the fringes, if only reeds, but the main problem is the open fresh water marsh. Most marshes are criss-crossed with dykes, and either these or the gates which mark the crossing points will give cover. An effective semi-permanent hide can be made from three stakes arranged in the form of a triangle with wire netting on two sides, and reeds or grass woven into the netting. A light temporary hide I sometimes carry is the three separated legs of a camera tripod, and a length of light muslin cloth dyed green. It is nearly always possible to contrive some form of hide, if only reeds woven in a barbed wire fence.

Wind is a help as the birds come in lower and more decisively, whereas on still nights they tend to circle. It has, however, the disadvantage that it muffles the sound of the duck wings which can normally be heard some seconds before the birds are visible. It is best to wait in the most convenient position possible for shooting, for if you are lying full length you will be spotted the instant you attempt to rise and the duck will have covered some way to safety before you are ready to fire. Duck which have been fired at tend to flee for the nearest water; a factor worth considering in selecting your position. When the moon is full, or nearly so, the duck may not flight until it rises, and then move throughout the night from feeding grounds to fresh water and back. On these nights the experienced gunners will be out both above and below the sea wall, the more so if there is a cover of thin cloud which makes the duck much more visible than the background of a clear sky.

Inland duck shooting will rarely give you a large bag but it may well provide you with some of your happiest hours with a gun.

Chapter 16

MOORLAND SHOOTING

As relatively few people are within easy reach of moorland shooting it may, at first thought, seem difficult to justify devoting a full chapter to this sport. In practice the easiest form of holiday shooting to find is the ground attached to the country hotels of the wilder areas of Scotland, Wales and Ireland, and my purpose in the next few pages is to firstly paint the scene, and secondly offer practical advice.

In spite of the population explosion we still enjoy very large areas of wild and extremely beautiful hill country, ranging from the almost total rock coverage of parts of Harris to the soft green loveliness of the Yorkshire Dales. In some areas the ground is efficiently keepered and provides superb driven grouse shooting of such quality that men will come from the corners of the earth and pay some hundreds of pounds each week for the sport. In others a combination of poor ground, vermin, excessive sheep stocks, and other factors means that sport is so sparse that the shooting rights can be had for very little, or even simply by asking. But inferior shooting does not mean inferior scenery – the sheer beauty of the hills remains. I have had many many happy hours with a gun, but none happier than those I have spent rough shooting in the West of Scotland. Here among the rocks, the heather, and the burns, you return to simple values where a yard of string becomes more valuable than a pound note, and a knob of cheese and cool water from the burn are more tasty than any business lunch. To walk knee deep through the blaze of August heather, and watch the sun strike diamonds on the deep blue of a hill loch; to feel the pull of the hill bite into the muscles of the legs; to listen to the distant croak of a raven on the still air, and watch a buzzard circle unendingly on set wings over the grey rocks – this is a unique and wonderful world and one which every shooting man should try to experience.

There are two ways of finding the ground. The first is to arrange a holiday in some remote spot and hope to find it when you arrive. This is not as chancy as it sounds, but still too risky if shooting is the sole purpose of the holiday. The second is to write to a variety of possible hotels to enquire if they have any shooting available. Success is certain if price is no object, for many hotels offer shooting. The problem comes if you can only afford a modest sum, and by this I mean say £5 to £25 a week for sport. It is highly unlikely that you will find anywhere in this category South of the Border, for the journey will be too easy for the big city dwellers. The secret is to write to the Scottish Tourist Board, at 2, Rutland Place, West End, Edinburgh, for a copy of *Where to stay in Scotland*, or alternatively to the Irish Tourist Office at 150 New Bond Street, London, W.1. Armed with these and a good map you can then prepare a list of likely places. There are very few which actually offer rough shooting at reasonable prices so you should write to small hotels in isolated spots and enquire if they either have, or can arrange, rough shooting. Avoid the larger hotels which boast of golf courses, swimming pools and tennis courts: they do not speak our language. Hotels which offer fishing are likely sources as they may have leased ground with the fishing rights.

Having succeeded in your quest and taken a first, slightly awed, look at the unending miles of apparently barren hills beware of applying the same techniques and equipment you would use for ordinary rough shooting. The advice that follows essentially refers to Scotland, but practically all of it holds good for moorland shooting anywhere in Britain. Rule one is to treat the hills with respect – they can and do kill. Today's colourful, quiet hillside, bathed in sun can tomorrow be swept by gale force winds and sheets of cold rain creating conditions so severe that a disabled man unable to reach shelter can be dead in hours. (It is not generally realized that even a fit man suffering from cold and fatigue and unable to reach shelter can die very quickly from hypothermia. This is the name for the condition in which the body loses heat faster than it can create it.) If you are going any appreciable distance from the roads always listen to the weather forecast, and leave a message detailing your route and when you expect to return. Ideally you should always have a companion. If you have and one of you is incapacitated the one who goes for rescue should leave his warm

▲31 Inland duck shooting—waiting by a flight line.

▼32 Moorland rough shooting in the Hebrides. Typical quarries for these surroundings are grouse, snipe, duck, hares and rabbits.

▲33 Grouse in flight. Walked up grouse are relatively easy targets.

▼34 Walking up grouse in good heather. Notice the shoulders are free of any weight and the cartridges, grouse and lightweight plastic coat are all at the waist.

clothing with the injured man, carefully check all land marks to facilitate his return, and place a shirt or some other conspicuous marker in a prominent spot by him. Unless the fit man is exhausted he should return with the rescue party to make sure they find the route at once.

A compass and a map are vital. You may be quite sure you do not need them at the start but if a mist comes down you will – and badly. Hill walking is hard work and nothing should be carried that is not strictly necessary. I find cartridges much more comfortable in a belt around my waist than in a bag on my shoulder. It is a good principle to carry no weight above waist level, and to leave the arms and shoulders free for the gun. With this principle in mind I never carry a game bag in the hills, but dangle the bag from the cartridge belt, Plate 34. Boots are practically a must for Wellingtons would be very tiring. On the warm August days shorts are much preferable to trousers, but avoid them if you will be walking through tall wiry old heather which will scratch badly. I would not bother to mention the infinitesimal risk of adders were it not for the fact that I missed stepping on one by a whisker a couple of years ago. If an adder should bite you take heart in the fact that the medical books say that it is almost unknown for its bite to kill a healthy adult. The remedy, they say, is not to cut above the bite and suck out the poison but to lie quietly. However, this hardly makes sense if you are some miles from the nearest human being. Personally I would set off walking slowly but steadily towards the nearest road. In the winter a waterproof jacket will be essential, but in August when the sun beats down and the heather dust rises in clouds at every footstep even a thin shirt is a burden. Provided the forecast is good on such days I take a cheap plastic macintosh rolled up into a tight bundle and hung from the belt.

As much of the pleasure comes from the scenery it is a bore to spend several hours meticulously working over a small area – far better to plan a long walk taking in a variety of habitats which in turn will give chances at a variety of quarries. To do this you need an Ordnance survey map of the area of not less than 1 inch to the mile, backed up by a preliminary reconnaissance which can often be done from a car with a pair of binoculars. Avoid walking aimlessly. A sample route might

9

start by an estuary and climb slowly over low boggy ground with the chance of snipe, rise to a large area of heather for grouse, rise once more to a high reed-fringed loch with a chance of duck, and finally drop down through bracken with rabbits. Ideally it is more fun if you can arrange to be picked up at a different spot from the starting place. Indeed the less energetic can be dropped in the hills and finish in a valley, thereby successfully spending most of the day walking down-hill. No matter how enthusiastic you may be if the weather forecast is for prolonged rain you will be wise not to start. Contrary to what some of the old writers would have us believe there is little pleasure to be found in walking in the hills in constant rain. Showery weather is another matter for it is usually possible to spot the showers looming in the distance and shelter in time. Overhanging rocks, peat hags, and even undercut river banks will give good cover, but you must carry warm clothing for the inactive spells. Also on showery days allow for covering a lesser distance.

On the type of ground where shooting may be had for little or nothing a belt of cartridges is usually ample. Typical quarries are duck and golden plover (but not before the 1st September) hares, rabbits, crows and hooded crows (but the latter two not both in the same area) blackcock, hill partridge, snipe and grouse. On occasions some thought must be given on whether to shoot or not. For example it would be foolish to shoot a hare if it then had to be carried for the next five hours. And it would be even more unwise to shoot at a snipe which rose close to a loch where you felt confident of finding duck. With fortune all these quarries may give you an opportunity but to my mind the most fascinating of them all is the grouse.

The grouse is a remarkable bird, unique to these Islands, and capable of surviving the cruellest of weather which will send even the red deer to the low ground. It lives mostly on the wiry green heather shoots, and if you try nibbling some you will see why the grouse has to grind up the heather within its crop with grit. The remote surroundings in which it lives, the call, habits, and colouring of the grouse all combine to give it a romantic, almost eerie, nature. Grouse are, in my view at least, the most difficult of all driven game birds, but walked up they are relatively easy. They make no attempt to gain height but burst from cover and skim off above the ground. The older birds are very clever at getting out of view behind the nearest undulation. The snag is not so much shooting them as finding them, and to succeed it is necessary to know something of their habits.

A pair of grouse will adopt a territory and will normally occupy this area with the covey they raise until it disperses. Although grouse will move from their home ground to the leeside of a hill to seek cover from strong winds the conditions must be very severe. What appears a strong wind to us standing 6 feet above the moor is merely a draught down among the heather at grouse level. However, grouse prefer a territory sheltered from the prevailing winds, and you will be wise to plan a route that takes this into account. A more important factor for grouse than weather is food, and although they do eat bilberries, grass seeds, and other oddments their staple diet is heather. If therefore you want to find the grouse you must go to the heather – and not just any heather but the right heather. This means heather which is old and tall enough to give cover but young enough still to be tender. Ideally it should not be an unbroken sea, but a sequence of islands of heather interspersed with short grasses which allow the grouse to move easily.

Obviously a dog is if not absolutely essential then nearly so. The usual common sense rules of rough shooting apply. The route should be planned into the wind if possible, and if not, across wind. Talking should be kept to bare essentials, for grouse will run considerable distances. Do not waste time covering an area minutely, for a covey will leave ample evidence of its presence. It is best to progress steadily, but to cover an area thoroughly once the dog reports a scent or you find fresh droppings and feathers. If the dog is obviously excited but cannot trace the covey they have either flown off unnoticed or are downwind. Height appears to make little difference to the presence or otherwise of grouse – I have found them both above the heather line, and almost at sea level. Nor should you head for the most isolated parts, for grouse have no objection to the reasonable presence of man.

When you fire at a covey reload immediately for the odd bird or two is often left behind and will rise after a few seconds. If a covey rises before you get in range watch them carefully for if not fired at they will sometimes drop within view or settle immediately they are out of sight. If you hit a bird which does not fall at once watch carefully until it is out of sight. Very often it will drop dead, and I have retrieved birds over half a mile distant. If it is hard hit it may settle immediately it is out of sight, and such birds are well worth following up. Winged birds that fall on open ground will run for the nearest thick cover and should be retrieved as quickly as possible. If there is a burn nearby they can often be found in the water and tucked under a bank.

Finally a plea for tolerance. Grouse in isolated areas have little experience of men, and, particularly if one or both of the parents is shot, will not fly far and often give you a chance to walk within range again. In fact a tenacious man could sometimes bag an entire covey. I feel very strongly that a brace from a covey is sufficient, and to take more is greedy. The true sportsman will find his covey, take a grouse or two and then leave them in peace.

Chapter 17

DRIVEN GAME SHOOTING

Driven game shooting is the more formal branch of shooting in which, as the name implies, the Guns remain stationary and the quarry is driven to them by beaters. This procedure can be practised with various quarries including snipe and partridges, but the vast majority of driven game shooting nowadays takes place at pheasant and grouse. Some of the shoots are privately owned and run, but many, and now-adays an increasing number, are syndicates. A century ago the syndicate was so little known that Richard Jeffries in *The Gamekeeper at Home* wrote 'The upper class of tradesmen in the country and provincial towns, where any facilities exist, now sometimes form a club or party, and rent the shooting over several farms, having a joint stock interest in one or more keepers'. With the passage of time the twin pressures of heavy taxation and increasing costs have made the syndicate the only possible solution for the man who has little time to spare for shooting, but a desire to enjoy a large bag without working over-hard for it. It is, of course, expensive, for the Guns have to share the rent of the shoot, sporting rates, keepers' wages, rearing costs, beaters' wages and a host of other outgoings. A Gun in a syndicate run on a shoe string with a part-time keeper and a modest bag may be had for a hundred pounds or so, but in a good and prolific shoot a Gun can cost many hundreds.

Driven game shooting is frequently criticized by practitioners of other forms of shooting on the grounds that its pursuit requires little or no fieldcraft, hardly any physical exertion, and is, in fact, simply a test of marksmanship. A further complaint is that it is a highly socialized activity in which a large slice of the day is spent talking and lunching. All this is true, but two points must be considered. Firstly, it is wrong to assume that a Gun at a formal shoot knows no fieldcraft; he may be a man with great experience of the countryside enjoying a day's driven shooting. Secondly if a man finds greater pleasure chatting to his fellow men and taking his sport easily rather than lying in the mud or fighting through brambles it is none of our business to criticize. In general the Guns at formal shoots tend to be older men, partly because they are more able to afford the cost, partly through a decrease in their physical powers, and, possibly most important, because as age mellows a man he is more interested in sharing the pleasure of being in the countryside with friends.

Many of the activities of shooting driven game are common to other forms of shooting, but various special considerations arise. First among these is safety.

Safety has been dealt with in detail in Chapter 6 but formal shoots bring special problems for there are so many people present: 35/40 is by no means unusual for the 8 Guns may well have 6 wives or friends, the keeper will have possibly 16 beaters and there may be 2 picker-ups, a stop, 2 drivers and someone bringing the lunch. In practice the presence of this minor army is not as dangerous as it first sounds for the activities of a formal shoot are well disciplined. At any well conducted shoot a signal, usually a whistle or horn, will announce the start and finish of each drive, and you must load and unload your gun at the appropriate time. Never load your gun, or, even worse, fire it between drives. Put simply, in a driven shoot the Guns form a line, spaced some 30 to 40 yards apart, facing some form of cover while the beaters advance in a straight line towards them. Not only have you to avoid shooting your neighbouring Guns and the advancing beaters, but it is common to place a picker-up or two behind the line and stops almost anywhere. A picker-up is a dog handler whose job it is to retrieve quickly any hard hit birds which come down well behind the line. A stop has to prevent birds running out of the cover along a hedge, ditch, or similar escape route. Faced with this great extent of danger angles there is only one rule for the less experienced – *never point your gun at a lesser angle than 45 degrees.* You may sometimes see a man wait for a rabbit to pass through the line and then shoot it, but he is either very experienced and quite certain of the location of everyone, or foolish. For the first few years you will be wise never to shoot at ground game in these circumstances. It should not be necessary to record that you should never swing your gun through the line so that it points at your neighbour, nor should you shoot a bird between you even if the angle of your gun is more than 45 degrees. Take it in front or behind, but not along the line. You will see this done, and without a murmur of protest, but by men who have shot together for years and have confidence in one another. As a beginner to driven game you must be ultra-cautious for, apart from the obvious need to avoid a tragedy, it is very easy for the newcomer to get a bad name for careless shooting when he is doing no more than some of the experienced Guns present. As the beaters move nearer so you must increase the angle below which you will not take a shot in front. Once the beaters are within range keep the barrels pointed skywards. All too frequently one can see a Gun who studiously avoids swinging through the line standing with his barrels pointing safely at the ground. But when a bird appears he will lift the barrels through the line of beaters to cover it, thereby committing the sin of swinging through the line on a vertical rather than a horizontal basis. Beware of holding your gun in the crook of your left arm so that your barrels cover your neighbour.

In older, stricter, times the host or syndicate captain would take a very firm line with any Gun offending the safety rules, sometimes ordering the culprit home. It is a pity that a more tolerant attitude now prevails in most shoots. It takes courage to reprimand a man, possibly much older than oneself, but it is the only way to forestall a possible tragedy.

Although a shooting party is usually formed of 8 Guns there may sometimes be 10. A brave, or alternatively thick-skinned, host will sometimes place the Guns himself, but the usual system is for the Guns to draw for numbers at the start of the day. The number one Gun will then take the position on the extreme right of the line as they face the beaters, and the last Gun will, of course, be on the extreme left. The positions are usually indicated by numbered pegs placed beforehand. For the second drive each Gun moves up two places, so the number one becomes number three and so on. When the party consists of 8 Guns the Gun who has just shot as number seven will move to number one for the next drive, and the number eight to number two. In practice the Guns shooting at the extreme flank positions will often be asked to walk level with the beaters. The purpose of varying numbers for each drive is to ensure, as far as possible, that each Gun gets a fair share of the sport, for obviously the central Guns get more sport than the flankers. Good manners dictate that you do not 'poach' your neighbour's birds. If it is nearer him than you leave it to him, and if equidistant let him fire first. If one of your neighbours persists in shooting your birds refrain from retaliating. Try to convince yourself that your forebearance is good for your character. If your companions are well-experienced you will notice they will decline to shoot low, slow, easy pheasants. You will do well to follow their example. Be very careful to memorize the number of birds you have down, and their location. Few things cause greater irritation to the organizers than the man who constantly thinks he had another one down but cannot remember where. Once you are placed avoid wandering, for your host not only knows better than you where the birds are likely to fly, but changing your position can be dangerous. If you have a dog make sure it is under control, and if it is not absolutely steady tie it to a peg by your feet while the drives are in progress. Do not let it seek a wounded bird in cover which has not yet been beaten without first getting permission; you may be putting it into the next drive. Make sure you have sufficient cartridges so that you avoid disturbing your neighbours for a loan during a drive. Play your part in helping to carry shot game to the game cart or a central point after each drive, unless it is obviously the practice to leave them to the hired hands. Make sure what you can and cannot shoot before the day starts. At many shoots partridges are now sacrosanct. In some areas you will get into hot water for shooting a fox, and in others you will be attacked if you let it through. At many shoots hen pheasants are not shot after Christmas, and you should check this.

Dress at driven game shoots is more formal than rough shooting. There is no set form but the rule is to turn out in neat but practical garb. Boots and plus two's will be more in evidence than Wellingtons and trousers, and heads will be crowned with caps or the Scotsman's 'fore and aft', rather than the wildfowler's traditional woollen ski hat. The sartorial effect at the beginning of the day is often quite splendid, but I am often amused when the arrival of rain brings out the waterproof clothing and reduces the whole team to a drab nondescript shapeless assembly.

Finally, tip the keeper, and speak well of the day, not only to him but the others. You may well be wet and miserable, but the organizers, who have laboured for months for this day, are much more depressed. A cheerful word of appreciation from you and the other Guns will help. The moaner may find his invitation to a private shoot is not renewed, or that the vacancy in a syndicate goes elsewhere. If you belong to a syndicate write to the captain at the end of each season with your thanks. Few men who have not done this exacting and usually honorary job realize how much effort goes to the common good. The question of how much to tip the keeper is not easily answered. Many people believe in relating this to the size of the bag, on the basis of £1 for every hundred. However the bag may be small through no fault of the keepers (possibly the standard of shooting!). It would have to be a modest shoot where a tip of £1 would be sufficient nowadays. The wisest course is quietly to seek the advice of a fellow Gun who has shot on the ground before.

The technique of shooting driven game follows basically the same principles of marksmanship as set out in Chapters 7 and 8, but with the difference that whereas in ordinary shooting the quarry may appear at any time and move in any direction with driven game you have the great advantage of knowing roughly when the birds will appear and where they will fly to. This advantage may vary from hearing a blast on the keeper's whistle five seconds before a pheasant appears, to staring over a barren moor for an hour when suddenly a covey of grouse appears from nowhere to flicker over your butt like ghosts. But whatever the extremes the Gun at a driven shoot knows when the drive has begun, where the birds are lying and where they will head when flushed. On the face of it his foreknowledge should make the task of hitting them much easier. In practice the high speed of most driven targets more than compensates for the Guns' initial advantage. In fact in my view driven grouse offer the most difficult, and most exciting, of all targets.

All good game shots make good use of this foreknowledge by getting to their peg or butt in good time and making sure they are fully ready before the targets appear. An essential ingredient of success is concentration, for shooting is an art and not a science and no artist ever painted a good picture or danced a ballet with his or her mind partly devoted to something else. A first step is to weigh up all the safety angles and engrave these in the mind; and not only as they are but as they will be when the beaters are close. Next ensure a good base for the feet, if necessary by stamping one out. Consider where you intend to kill the birds, and position your feet accordingly. Actions like this contribute towards neat, tidy shooting and it is noticeable that whereas the novice often appears to be flailing his body and barrels in all directions the experienced shot often does no more than move his barrels slightly. This is largely due to the fact that he was in the right position before the target appeared. I earlier warned of ensuring that you start with an ample supply of cartridges, and that an unreliable dog is tethered – strictly speaking it should not be there at all. A further preliminary is to silence a talkative companion. The right clothing for the day is important, for no man can shoot to his best standard if he is wet or cold. This is also the moment for checking the direction and strength of the wind, for a strong side wind will cause a bird to drift considerably. The absence of fixed landmarks in the sky will make this drift difficult to detect, but it will be quite enough to cause a miss. If your observations suggest drifting will be likely, watch for it carefully, and swing on the downwind wing tip and not the body. This has the effect of giving a sideways lead at the same instant that you are providing for forward lead.

In rough shooting the Gun very rarely has the choice of the angle at which to shoot the quarry but with driven game you can, within the limits of safety, shoot it in front, behind, or at any point in between. Indeed at some shoots where the standard is not high you will see birds taken over a wide range of angles. In fact there is a cardinal rule for shooting driven game - *take them well out in front.* There are two reasons for this. Firstly the targets speed in relation to the path of the shot is slower than when directly overhead, and less lead is necessary (if the reason is not clear consider the extreme case of the bird low in front which requires no lead at all). Secondly if the first barrel misses the second can be taken at a sensible angle instead of almost falling over backwards. This latter factor also helps towards achieving right and lefts when the opportunities occur. If you watch other Guns in action you will see how late the indifferent shots leave their first barrel in contrast to the experts, who rap the target smartly under the chin at 45 degrees. As a broad rule you should try to drop the birds in front, or at least at your feet. If they fall far behind you are almost certainly leaving your shot too late.

One of the joys of formal shooting is the old gentlemen who sit precariously on their shooting sticks, apparently in an advanced state of senility, only to spot and shoot anything that comes near. I have happy memories of an old man at a Hampshire shoot who when we were introduced extended only two fingers of his right hand explaining that he had mild paralysis. At the first drive all the birds were destined to cross his front before reaching me, and I expected a good harvest. 'You stop them for me boy' he wheezed 'I shan't hit them'. There were nine, and he killed the lot. He, and others of his ilk, have perfected the knack of waiting in any casual posture, but the beginner is well advised to wait in a 'ready' position. I suggest you grip the butt between the biceps of the shooting arm and your chest, and raise the barrels until they point skywards at 45 degrees or so. The hands should be in their final shooting positions. From then on the procedure set out in Chapter 7 in Marksmanship applies.

Remember that the great temptation for the novice is to mount the gun, and then chase the target across the sky in a series of small jerks, each intended to correct minor errors of aim. This is usually fatal, for it leads to poking. The need is to be decisive. Decide where you are going to kill the bird, be firm, bold and shoot. If you miss in front you could be a competent shot out of form – miss behind and you are obviously a duffer. Probably there is no branch of live shooting where practice at clay pigeons is so helpful as driven game. Given a competent instructor you should have the knack of taking approaching birds in the first dozen or so clays, and once you have it it is with you for life.

Many men claim that one of the most difficult birds is that sighted a long way off, and advise looking away until it is nearer. But this throws your advantage of having time to assess your shot. The reason these birds are missed is not that their long viewing hypnotizes the Gun, but that he is tempted to begin his gun mounting sequence prematurely, and thereby destroying his timing. The secret is to look at the bird from the beginning but to delay physical movement until it can flow smoothly and without interruption. Perhaps the old gentlemen owe more to their shooting sticks and stiff joints than they realize.

Chapter 18

GUNDOGS
THEIR TRAINING AND HANDLING

It is possible to shoot without the assistance of a dog. In fact years ago I wrote an article offering advice to sportsmen in this position entitled *The Dogless Gun* (my wittier friends suggested a follow up called *The Gunless Dog*). However, there are very good reasons why a dog is, to say the least, highly desirable.

First and foremost are humane considerations. There is an obligation on every sportsman to avoid wounding his quarry if he possibly can, but occasionally a wounded bird or animal gets into cover and without a dog the chances of finding it are poor. A good dog will make recoveries from considerable distances and will practically eliminate the unpleasant business of leaving badly wounded creatures. Secondly the rough shooter will enjoy more sport – in some cases much more. In reasonably thick cover many of the quarries will prefer to hide rather than flee, and the dogless gun walks past much more than he realizes. A dog also increases the bag by its ability to retrieve those items which the sportsman would have missed, either because they fell in thick cover or across water. They may well have been cleanly killed but they will never reach the larder and have died for no purpose. A further reason that seems not to occur to the non-dog owners is that it is selfish to shoot regularly with friends who have dogs if you have not. They have had the considerable trouble and expense of buying, training and maintaining the beasts so why should you take it for granted that they will flush most of your chances for you, and then retrieve them if you cannot readily find them. The last reason is pure sentiment but for many dog owners it is one of the most important. A dog is a great companion and brings to the day all the enthusiasm of a keen boy. One moment almost exploding with scarcely contained excitement, head erect, eyes bright, standing stiff legged with nose to the breeze; the next covering ground fast on a hot scent with ears flying. A man, a dog, and his gun share many experiences together, and once you have shot for a season with a dog you will never be without one. Some years ago my spaniel was killed by a lorry when a wounded cock she was seeking doubled back and crossed a lane. It was weeks before I wanted to shoot again, and the next season before I felt the old enthusiasm. But by then I had a new dog.

So having stressed the need for a dog let me briefly describe what the ideal dog does for his shooting master. Whilst remaining under complete control it searches all the ground thoroughly, but never quests beyond the range of the gun. It will flush, but not chase, whatever it finds, and when you shoot it will sit, or at least remain quite still. On command it will retrieve from land and water, and do so gently without crushing the quarry. In practice its activities will no doubt also include fighting with your companions dogs, jumping on your car seat with muddy paws, pinching your sandwich lunch when you are not looking and numerous similar vices. Finally it will love you more than any other living thing in the world.

The chance that you will ever own such a paragon of virtue as that described at the beginning of the last paragraph is remote, for it is difficult enough for a full-time professional trainer to achieve this standard with almost unlimited time. For the inexperienced amateur with a job to do, and possibly a car journey before he reaches suitable ground, it is well nigh impossible. You may well read books on the subject that suggest I am wrong, but unless you are prepared to make dog training the central interest in your life it cannot be done. The proof of this statement is the overwhelming number of incompletely trained dogs one sees, and the very, very few really good ones. What I have done, and I suggest you do, is to bring a dog to the best level that time and ability permits, and then rest content. When she sometimes sins I refuse to get heated – if I really want to eliminate them then I must give up some other interest and concentrate on dog training. It is important to train your dog as well as you possibly can, but it is also important not to ruin your day by getting over excited when things go wrong. There are worse problems in life.

One solution to the task of dog training is either to buy a trained dog or send yours away for training. This is expensive, but if you adopt this course you must be aware of two factors. Firstly a dog which has been trained by one man will not work as well for a second without some rehearsals. Secondly no matter how well a dog has been trained it will become rusty if merely left in a basket to snooze until each shooting day comes round. Getting a dog into a high pitch of training, and keeping it there, requires constant exertion. It is senseless to aim at a higher level than you can maintain.

I hope I have made you at least slightly aware of both the problems and joys of dog ownership, and you may now be seriously thinking of buying a puppy to train. If so I would ask you not to do this lightly. In so many cases a dog is a novelty, fussed over by everyone for a few weeks. Then it can easily become a nuisance, neglected and unwanted. If you are an absolute beginner to shooting I suggest you defer buying a dog until you have had a season's experience. After all if you have no practical experience of shooting you can hardly teach a dog what to do, and if your interest in the sport flags then you are not faced with a dog looking at you in the expectation of an outing.

Assuming you are sure of your continuing interest and have some experience of shooting, the question of the best breed arises. There is no 'best' breed for all men – it depends on your most frequent form of shooting and the ground you cover. There are many varieties which *can* be used for shooting (my wife's poodle has an excellent nose) but there is no reason to go beyond the two most popular breeds – the labrador retriever and the springer spaniel. The labrador is probably the easier to train being quieter and more tractable, and he is also by virtue of his size the stronger swimmer, but the general view is that spaniels are the more natural hunters. Their smaller size also makes it easier for them to work thick cover. In general I would suggest that for wildfowling, formal driven game shooting (where the dog's only work is retrieving) and possibly rough shooting in open areas, the labrador is best; but for all-round rough shooting the spaniel wins. Certainly the spaniel is more fun. The behaviour of a spaniel when you appear in the right clothes and carrying a gun case brings joy to the heart.

Having decided on the breed you favour it is vital to buy a puppy from a good working strain. There are only two safe ways. One is to buy from a reputable breeder, and the other from a litter where you have personally witnessed the mother working and the father is from a good working strain, or vice versa. The experts can talk for hours about pedigrees, but for we ordinary mortals a good scattering of Field Trial Champions in the pedigree must be sufficient reassurance. Unquestionably the safest course is to buy from a dealer but it will also be the most expensive.

The practically universal mistake that all novice trainers make is to work their dog under actual shooting conditions too quickly. A young dog is not unlike a young child – until it matures to the point where it can avoid getting over excited it is liable to lose control. Once this happens the task of re-training is far harder than the original job of training. I believe a partial explanation for the enormous number of incompletely controlled dogs seen in the shooting field is that they were worked too soon. Nor am I blameless. When I lost my last spaniel I was so anxious not to shoot without a dog that I started the present spaniel prematurely. She is a good dog, but she could have been a better one.

This warning is against working dogs too soon – not against beginning training too early. Elementary training can begin at a few months, the only point to watch being that you do not bore the dog with long repetitive sessions. Make no attempt to teach a puppy anything but the basics; these are to walk to heel, to sit, and to come when called. If you can train your dog invariably to perform these three actions then you have made great progress towards the finished article. Teach your dog to walk by your left side if you are right handed and will be carrying your gun over the right arm. Start with the dog on a lead, and jerk it back, fairly sharply, whenever he transgresses. When it is keeping by you satisfactorily dispense with the lead and cut a light switch from a hedge. This is not for beating the poor beast, but touching lightly on the head or flank if it starts to creep ahead or angle away.

Coming to call is best taught at the beginning by giving a tit-bit as reward, but this should be dispensed with as soon as possible. Digressing, for a moment, I think it is a mistake to control a gun dog by voice as in rough shooting the sound of the human voice will clear

▲35 Beaters on a frosty morning. This pheasant has risen from a field of kale but is heading for the flank rather than towards the waiting Guns.

▼36 Waiting at a grouse butt. The thin sticks are to remind the Gun not to swing through the line.

▲37 Driven pheasant at a Hampshire shoot. The second Gun has shot the bird at the right place—well out in front—and its legs have already dropped.

▼38 The author's springer spaniel retrieving an English partridge.

the ground of all wild life for some considerable distance. It is wisest to train your dog to a whistle, or preferably two. One can be used to give the order to sit, and the other, according to the way it is used, the remaining commands. I suggest using one whistle only for the command sit, because this is the most important instruction you will give your dog.

There are few more laughable, or depressing, depending on the part you play, sights than a man incessantly blowing his whistle at a dog which ignores him. The only way to teach your dog to respond to the first call is to blow the whistle just once. If it fails to respond do not blow again but wait until you eventually catch it. Lead it back to the point where it transgressed, then blow the whistle and pull it firmly towards you. You must learn to think like a dog, and to appreciate that the thinking powers of a dog are very limited. I have seen a man whose dog has ignored his recall whistle go on blowing until the dog has eventually returned, at which stage he has beaten it. In the eyes of the dog it has just been beaten for going to its master when he whistled it. If a dog is to be punished it must be obvious to it just what the punishment is for. This means delivering the punishment as quickly as possible after the offence, *and at the precise spot*. If you cannot be certain that the dog connects the punishment with the offence it is better to do nothing. Additionally the degree of punishment varies from dog to dog. Personally I find that speaking to the dog in an angry voice is sufficient in most cases. I have never gone beyond shaking a dog roughly while holding it by the loose skin of the neck, but I am sure many more competent trainers than I would advocate tougher measures occasionally.

It is important to keep to a minimum the opportunities for a dog to do wrong or misunderstand. Most dogs are very anxious to please if only they know what they are supposed to do. As a simple example consider the art of training a dog to come to call. If you start with the dog held by somebody only a few yards away, and whistle and gesture to it when its attention is fully fixed on you then it is practically certain to come. Conversely if the dog is a hundred yards away the risk that it will not even start towards you, or become bored or discover a fascinating scent on the way, is far higher.

Teaching the dog to sit is a simple, if somewhat boring procedure. The command you use can be 'sit', 'drop', 'down', or for that matter 'cough drops'; all that counts is that you use precisely the same command every time. As I mentioned earlier I prefer a whistle, and if you follow suit this should be used from the very beginning. An extended arm, with hand open, palm down, is a useful visual signal to accompany the whistle. At the beginning you will have to be near the dog, and it will almost certainly be necessary to make it sit by pressing its hind quarters down firmly. Once it sits consistently the next stage is to keep it there while you walk away. At first you will back away only a yard or two before it is up. It is essential to take it firmly back to the precise point it has left, and sit it once more. When it will remain consistently then teach it to remain even though you pass from its sight. The next stage is to train it to sit wherever it is, and whatever it is doing whenever you command it, and if this lesson is well and truly drilled home you have made a major step towards a good gundog. There are many occasions in a day's shooting when it is necessary to stop a dog; it may be working at extreme range, moving near to cover which is not to be worked until later, or simply looking longingly at a fleeting hare. To be able to cause it to sit and look for instructions with just a quick peep on the whistle is an obvious advantage.

So far we have concerned ourselves with the negative actions of preventing the dog from following its natural instincts, but eventually it has to be taught to hunt. If the dog comes from a good working strain hunting will be instinctive, and your real task is teaching it to hunt sufficiently near to you so that game flushed is within range. Some trainers use a check cord, which is simply a long length of cord which allows them to restrain the dog whenever it moves too far from them. This is theoretically excellent, but from a practical angle difficult unless the ground is very open. The advantage of having a dog obedient to the whistle before it hunts freely is obvious.

On a typical training walk with a young dog I would keep it to heel at the start, and return it to heel at intervals. In between it would be encouraged to work out suitable cover, but always keeping reasonably close. I would not let it follow its own whims for more than a moment or so, but constantly instruct it. The dog has to realize that its job is to watch for and obey orders. This means recalling it, sending it to investigate a particular piece of cover, signalling it to right or left, whistling it to sit, waving it on again – a constant stream of simple instructions, firmly given, and with an insistence on complete obedience.

This is the stage at which a dummy can be introduced, for it is a mistake for a dog's first retrieve to be of the real thing. I use a piece of soft wood, well bound with carpet felt, and covered with a rabbit skin. At the beginning the dog should be sat, the dummy tossed a few yards, and when, and only when, you wave the dog to retrieve, it will almost certainly run to investigate. With any luck the instinct of the centuries will cause it to pick up the dummy whereupon you blow the recall on the whistle. This may not work the first time, but retrieving is one of the things most dogs do well, and certainly teaching it to retrieve is far easier than teaching it to sit in the face of temptation. When the dog returns with the dummy do not be in a hurry to take it. Make the dog sit, then hold the dummy gently and encourage the dog to release it. Never, never engage in a tugging match or the dog will develop hard mouth, a term used to describe a dog who holds game so viciously that it damages it. A good dog will retrieve an egg without cracking it.

Once the dog retrieves well there are variations of dummy training. The dummy can be hidden in cover when the dog is not looking, and then the cover worked until the dummy is found. This also encourages a dog to hunt. A useful memory trainer is to place the dummy on the ground within sight of the dog, and then call it to heel and walk away. After 50 yards the dog will be sent back for the dummy, and each day the distance can be increased. Any activity which keeps the dog alert, and encourages obedience is good, but beware of boring the dog. Half a dozen retrieves in any one training session will do.

There are many opportunities for training within the home. For example if you can train a young dog to sit until released when its food is put down you may later stand some chance when a rabbit gets up under its nose. Professionals and keepers usually keep their dogs in kennels, but this situation is forced upon them by sheer weight of numbers. Not only is there no objection to keeping a gundog indoors, but the closer association this permits can be all for the good of both dog and master.

It is not over difficult, although it takes time and patience, to get a dog to a high stage of obedience with the simple disciplines I have outlined. But disaster usually strikes when the owner decides that training is over and work must begin. The transition from training runs in quiet surroundings with one familiar human to a shooting day with many different people, smells, and other dogs, all moving excitedly to the noise of guns, and with a variety of real game to be retrieved is simply too much. The poor beast forgets most of its training and goes back to puppyhood. The first gun a dog hears should be fired several hundred yards away, and gradually it can be brought nearer. For the first few shoots, and preferably for the first season, a dog should attend shooting days purely as an observer from the side of its master. An occasional retrieve during a quiet moment is permissible, but any attempt to hunt a dog in the first few outings will inevitably cause trouble. Gradually it will grow accustomed to the new experiences, and show less excitement. Then you can work it quietly, checking constantly that it responds to the 'sit' whistle. If it disobeys then back it must go on the lead until it has learnt discretion. A young inexperienced dog should never be sent to retrieve wounded game or in the struggle it may kill the creature and become permanently addicted to this sin.

One mark of a well trained dog is its ability to 'drop to shot'. This means that on hearing the report of a gun it drops, or at least sits, and awaits orders rather than running in to retrieve the quarry which may or may not have fallen. As with the other aspects of training this can be taught from an early age, but do heed my earlier warning against firing a gun too close to the dog before it has grown used to what is an alarming noise. For this reason an assistant is needed at the start to fire the gun while you oblige the dog to drop on the report. It is relatively easy to teach dropping to shot whilst training, but surprisingly hard to maintain the discipline under actual shooting conditions. This illustrates the much stiffer task that faces the man who trains a dog to seek and flush game as distinct from the man who simply trains a dog to retrieve it. The task of controlling a dog which spends most of its time sitting beside a shooting stick and rarely enjoying much freedom is far easier than with an animal who is constantly sent exploring the undergrowth and is out of its master's sight for half the time.

I hope you will not read into this last comment, or indeed the chapter generally, a suggestion that you should be content with an indifferent performance from your dog. For reasons which are too obvious to need detailing you should achieve the highest standard of training possible. But having said this I would ask you to bear the word 'possible' in mind, and remind you of the philosophy I expounded at the start of this chapter. There is a limit to what an otherwise busy man, working with a dog which is unlikely to be better than average, can achieve. Having reached this limit do not be too depressed if the results fall rather short of perfection – you are in good company.

Over the years numerous men have filled large books on the subject of training gundogs, and in one brief chapter I have only been able to give scanty advice. If you train a dog of your own you will be wise to study the problems in greater detail and I recommend you purchase *Spaniels for Sport*, a re-edited version by Talbot Radcliffe of H. W. Carlton's outstanding book on the breaking of spaniels. The publishers are Faber & Faber who also publish this book.

Chapter 19

COOKING THE QUARRY

All shooting and fishing men will tell you that whatever you have captured yourself acquires a magical taste. This is delightfully true, but too many sporting books which have gone into minute detail in telling you how to reduce the unfortunate creature to hand assume that the reader has some inborn instinct on cooking, for the subject is ignored. This chapter sets out to remedy this gap, even though it may be the moment of time when this book passes from the hands of the man who has followed me loyally for 18 chapters into those of his wife.

As the majority of your quarry are likely to be birds I will deal with these first and hares and rabbits later. In many cases where the bag is small you will have little or no chance to be selective, but where a choice exists always, for obvious reasons, pick young birds. In some cases selection is easy; for example an old cock pheasant has long sharply pointed spurs whereas the spurs of a young cock are blunt and short; and with grouse the third primary feather of a young bird is shorter than those adjoining, the lower beak will not support the weight of the body, and the skull is easily crushed. These differences become increasingly hard to detect as the season progresses. In all birds the young are characterized by having softer more even feathers than the old. Firm plump breasts and smooth pliable legs are other points to look for.

Most birds require hanging for a while or their flesh is tough and tasteless. This does not apply to duck whose flesh quickly becomes rank; two or three days is quite enough for them. Birds should be hung by the neck without plucking or drawing, and the time will vary with the weather and individual tastes. In warm weather a week will be enough, and in cold conditions two or even three weeks is acceptable. In the later summer and early autumn birds should be hung away from flies, and at all times in a cool, dry, airy place. Snipe and woodcock require less hanging than other game birds.

You will be more popular if you avoid plucking birds indoors, but in any event keep away from a draught and spread a newspaper to catch the feathers. Pluck several feathers at a time, and pull towards the head – that is against the natural lie. Be careful to avoid tearing the skin, and if this happens take fewer feathers at a time. Personally I do not bother with the wings beyond the first joint as the extra meat obtained is insufficient to warrant the bother. Once plucked singe, that is burn off, the hairs, by holding the bird over a small naked flame and turning quickly.

It is not usual to remove the sinews from the legs, and the feet are left on. However, when entertaining town dwellers who are not accustomed to eating meat in any form in which the original beast can be recognized it is best to remove the feet. For these sensitive souls the less the meal looks like a bird the better. Remove the head by first cutting the skin some 2 inches up the neck from the body. Roll the skin down and then cut through the neck as close to the body as possible. This leaves an ample fold of skin which will not shrink sufficiently to expose the breast meat when cooking begins. Slit up the stomach for about 2 inches from the vent, but avoid cutting the intestines. Very gently insert two fingers and remove the entrails, taking care not to miss the heart and lungs which are well forward. The cookery books all tell one to wipe the interior with a clean damp cloth. I do not, because I believe it to be unnecessary, a view re-inforced by the fact that snipe and woodcock are not drawn at all.

Strictly speaking, birds should be trussed, with the object of maintaining the shape so that it will be easy to carve. I do not always bother. The experts use a trussing needle, but a skewer and fine string will do. Place the bird on its breast, and push the skewer through just below the thigh bone. Then pass the string under the ends of the skewer and cross it over the back, at the same time catching in the wing pinions. Turn the bird onto its back, and tie the ends of the string together around the tail, and at the same time secure the drum sticks.

There are several ways in which game can be cooked, and many more different accompaniments, garnishings and flavourings, but the more simply the job is done the better. Older, and therefore tougher, birds can be stewed, casseroled or braised, but for young birds roasting is best. The breast should be covered with bacon to compensate for the lack of fat in game birds, and then basted regularly with butter or margerine. Roasting times will naturally vary with the size of the bird and the temperature of the oven, but in a moderately hot oven a partridge or teal will take 20 to 30 minutes, a grouse 30 to 45 minutes, and a pheasant about an hour. A thin gravy and fried crumbs are normal accompaniments. Bread sauce, and often green salad, are served with pheasant, partridge and grouse, and orange salad with duck.

Pigeons need ample cooking and are better stewed or casseroled slowly rather than roasted. If you have a good supply it is best simply to remove the breasts rather than go through the mess and labour of plucking whole pigeons for very little more meat. Once again the meat is dry, and fat bacon should be included in the stew or casserole.

Rabbits should be eaten as soon as possible, but hares should be hung by the rear legs, and, like game, the period will depend on the weather. Keen housewives catch the blood by hanging a pot under the head and using it for gravy. Rabbits should be paunched as soon as possible – hares left until they are prepared for cooking. To paunch a rabbit or hare slit up the stomach from the crutch to the ribs, cutting only through the pelt and inner skin. Turn the animal's stomach down on a newspaper to allow gravity to assist in removing the entrails. Remove also the various organs, keeping the kidneys, and, if the cook so wishes, the heart and liver. Cut off the feet at the first joint. Separate the pelt from the inner skin on both sides of the slit made in the stomach, and work the fingers between the two layers until they meet at the back. Now continue working towards the rear until the back can be flexed and the pelt pulled, inside out, over the rear legs until they are free. It then becomes a simple matter to pull the pelt and the body apart until they have separated as far as the neck, which is cut to remove the head. The pelt then pulls over the front legs, leaving the body ready for jointing. Cut off the legs, leaving as much flesh as possible on the legs and not the body. Chop or cut the back into convenient lengths.

Hares and rabbits may be boiled, stewed, casseroled, or jugged, and served in a wide variety of ways from curried rabbit, through rabbit *à l'italiène*, to the more conventional rabbit hot-pot.

The most usual treatment for a rabbit is stewing, and the first step is to fry the portions, first dipping them in seasoned flour. Mushrooms and onions are also fried, and all go into the stewpan with stock, and herbs. This should be brought to the boil, then allowed to simmer when the vegetables are added. Simmering continues for at least 1½ hours, until the flesh is tender.

Although all the ways of cooking rabbits can be applied to hares the traditional, and highly successful, method is jugged. Take a casserole, and, using dripping fry the joints in it with bacon. Add stock, blended flour, and a muslin bundle of onions, herbs and seasoning. Cook gently in a moderate oven until tender, which will be about 3 hours. Remove the muslin bundle, and serve with redcurrant jelly.

INDEX